LAST TRAIN HOME

THE DISAPPEARANCE OF KRYSTAL FRASER

DENNIS O'BRYAN

Published in Australia by Sid Harta Books & Print Pty Ltd,
ABN: 34632585293
23 Stirling Crescent, Glen Waverley, Victoria 3150 Australia
Telephone: +61 3 9560 9920, Facsimile: +61 3 9545 1742
E-mail: author@sidharta.com.au

First published in Australia 2023
This edition published 2023
Copyright © Dennis O'Bryan 2023

Cover design: Heath McCurdy
Typesetting: WorkingType (www.workingtype.com.au)

The right of Dennis O'Bryan to be identified as the Author of the Work has been asserted in accordance with the Copyright, Designs and Patents Act 1988.

All rights reserved. No part of this publication may be reproduced, stored in a retrieval system, or transmitted, in any form or by any means without the prior written permission of the publisher, nor be otherwise circulated in any form of binding or cover other than that in which it is published and without a similar condition being imposed on the subsequent purchaser.

Dennis O'Bryan
Last Train Home
ISBN: 978-1-922958-10-5

Disclaimer: The author has made every effort to ensure that the information in this book was correct at the time of publication and assumes full and sole responsibility for the contents which have been gathered and written in the public interest. All information is the result of the author's own research, investigations and interviews with all persons mentioned and quoted. Some names and identifying details have been changed to protect the privacy of individuals and this is noted in all instances where this has occurred. Any opinions expressed are solely those of the author, unless otherwise indicated.

ABOUT THE AUTHOR

Dennis O'Bryan grew up on a farm in rural Victoria and joined Victoria Police at eighteen.

He completed twenty-seven years as an operational police officer, with uniform and plain clothes duties.

During his policing career, in which he rose to the rank of inspector, Dennis received nine commendations/citations, two of them for bravery but the majority for running successful protracted criminal investigations. He has post graduate qualifications in public policy and administration.

Following his police career, he owned and operated holiday parks in Swan Hill. He is now retired and enjoys solo multi-day bush walks.

Last Train Home, a true crime investigation, is his first book.

DEDICATION

*To the memory of Krystal,
who just wanted to be loved.*

ACKNOWLEDGEMENTS

I wish to thank everyone who was prepared to speak to me during my research for this book. Talking about Krystal was difficult for a number of people and their participation illustrates the local community's genuine desire to solve the mystery of Krystal's disappearance.

Of course, without access to Krystal's family my book would not exist:

Karen Fraser, Krystal's mum, while initially very reluctant to speak to me, essentially provided me with a pathway for the book. Her openness and raw honesty helped me to know and understand Krystal. The lengthy conversations I had with Karen in her dining room were contrasted by tears, laughter, and anger, but not regret, as she was confident she had helped Krystal live a happy life. Karen was responsible for keeping the family together during the early stages of the investigation when rumours and innuendo hinted that Karen and husband Neil may have been involved in their daughter's death. She also took responsibility for dealing with police and media and administering the Facebook page ('Help us find Krystal Fraser') she developed with daughter Chantel in an effort to provide answers.

Krystal's father Neil, an outwardly tough guy, struggled

badly with the thought that someone could kill Krystal. By his own admissions he became reclusive, spending many years working and living the majority of the week in Melbourne. That said, he welcomed and assisted my efforts in trying to discover what happened to his daughter.

Krystal's younger sister, Chantel (Tilly) who lives interstate, has been a tremendous help in locating potential witnesses and setting up interviews for me. She spent a great deal of time carrying out her own investigation after Krystal's disappearance and had established many contacts that she shared with me for my investigation. She was also my bullshit detector, diverting me from wasting time on useless bits of information.

My mate and former police colleague Bob Kerr and his wife Kim helped with brainstorming episodes during periods of doubt to keep me on track. Bob also assisted with a couple of interviews during my research. I appreciate them for their friendship and support throughout.

My elder sister Margaret provided an impartial and pertinent critique of my first draft and helped me to see the big picture.

My daughter Clare, the smartest and most resilient woman I know, made time for proofreading and editing and, like my sister, was not shy in her feedback.

My wife Di has supported and encouraged me throughout and I owe her profoundly.

I also wish to thank those cops who provided snippets

of intelligence along the way in support of a resolution to the investigation, albeit that they did so in breach of their employer's constraints. They will remain anonymous.

CONTENTS

Chapters

One	*Krystal's final hours*	1
Two	*Missing*	10
Three	*Initial police response*	18
Four	*Role of Senior Constable Jason Brady*	26
Five	*Preservation of the Scene*	46
Six	*Criminal Investigation Unit Involvement*	56
Seven	*A Homicide Squad Investigation*	66
Eight	*Pyramid Hill*	75
Nine	*The Frasers*	83
Ten	*Krystal Lee Fraser*	99
Eleven	*Krystal's Interactions*	108
Twelve	*Why Kill?*	118
Thirteen	*Reward Inducement*	124
Fourteen	*Jason McPherson*	129
Fifteen	*Investigation Hiatus*	137
Sixteen	*Stephen Hugh Jones (Deceased)*	143
Seventeen	*Craig 'Twiggy' Newton*	156
Eighteen	*Sting Operation Targeting Newton*	171
Nineteen	*Covert Operation Aftermath*	183
Twenty	*Peter Jenkinson — 'PJ'*	193
Twenty-One	*Missing Persons Squad*	217

Twenty-Two	*Peter Jenkinson's Relationships*	225
Twenty-Three	*McGillivray Abattoirs*	239
Twenty-Four	*Where Is Krystal?*	246
Twenty-Five	*Coronial Inquest*	255
Twenty-Six	*Conclusion*	267

CHAPTER ONE

Krystal's final hours

Krystal Lee Fraser, twenty-three years of age, was an outpatient in the maternity accommodation section of the Bendigo Hospital awaiting the birth of her first child, a son she planned to name Ryan. It was Saturday 20 June 2009. She had been conveyed there the previous night by ambulance from her tiny flat in Pyramid Hill, a minor pastoral town of about four hundred residents eighty-six kilometres north of Bendigo.

Krystal had called the ambulance just as she had been instructed to by health workers. They had told her if she felt pain or a squeezing of her stomach these were contractions that meant her baby was on the way. Krystal knew these instructions were important because she had no means of getting herself to hospital and there were no local hospitals. She also knew that if she left the call too late the baby could be born on the way.

Luckily for Krystal, Zelma Doyle, a member of the local community emergency response team, known as CERT, who lived directly across the street, attended in response to the emergency call and told Krystal she was in fact having contractions.

Zelma was surprised to see Krystal home on the Friday night as she had also attended to her earlier that week when Krystal had been similarly conveyed to Bendigo to have her baby. She guessed that had been a false alarm. It was a bit hard to tell with Krystal. She had been born with an undiagnosed foetal brain injury or an inherited genetic abnormality which had resulted in a condition formerly known as congenital hydrocephalus, or 'fluid on the brain'– as it is commonly referred to. The disorder, whatever the cause, meant that Krystal had an intellectual disability.

It was clear to Zelma, who had a nursing background, that this impacted on some of Krystal's decision-making but she knew that the young woman did the best she could. She thrived in her small local community and had lived independently for the past four years. Krystal knew the town and its people, and everyone knew her. She lived within walking distance of everything she needed. She was a regular at the pub. She was a fan of the Pyramid Hill footy club and went to games to cheer on the Bulldogs. She loved riding the VLine train as it fulfilled her sense of adventure and provided an escape from her limited surroundings. It seemed to those around her, she was always on the move, always up for a chat.

While many assumed Krystal was living her best life, she had one vulnerability. Men. Krystal was blonde, slim and, although she had completed Year 12, she was seen as socially

Chapter One Krystal's final hours

awkward, not good at reading social cues. Krystal trusted people, but particularly men, because they would have fun with her when most women wouldn't. But the trust Krystal afforded others was based on her own sense of trust — *I will do the right thing by you and you will treat me the same.* This combination of naivety and unguarded trust made her vulnerable to the attentions of men who showed an interest in her. Her contraception implant, fitted nine months earlier, had failed. Hence the imminent arrival.

The labour scare resulting in her latest ambulance trip to hospital had not led to the birth of her baby and Krystal was bored and restless on the Saturday. Around lunchtime she told nurse David Reed that she was considering returning to Pyramid Hill for a party. David told her he thought this was a bad idea as she was due to have her baby and booked in to be induced on the following Tuesday if it had not been born by then.

Krystal approached the nurses' station a couple of hours later and again raised the possibility of returning home; this time nurse Jenny Rendall was also present. David appreciated that Krystal was more determined to go on this occasion. As a result, a call was made to the maternity wing where the nurses' concerns about Krystal's planned departure were discussed.

David was surprised when her release was approved. He said he questioned Krystal further about the party and was relieved to learn that Krystal would be among friends and the party was to celebrate a friend's birthday.

David felt that Krystal was more interested in the party than her advanced state of pregnancy, although both nurses indicated that Krystal was excited about the pending birth. Telstra records show that Krystal received a phone call on her mobile at 5.42 that afternoon, while still at the hospital. Hearing later of the circumstances of Krystal's departure, members of the Fraser family were disturbed that any kind of release was sanctioned. Krystal assured the nurses that she would catch the first train back the next morning as it was impossible for her to return that night. She was going and was subsequently granted a night pass. As far as Krystal was concerned, Saturday nights were for partying and she wasn't about to knock back an invitation. It wasn't as if she got a lot. That she was due to give birth was not as significant to her as the invitation.

When nurse Jenny Reed returned to the hospital after making outpatient home visits she checked Krystal's room and saw that the clothes Krystal had been wearing earlier were on the bed. All Krystal's other possessions, including her medications, were in an open suitcase on the floor. Amongst these belongings was a stuffed teddy bear that Krystal had excitedly told her was a present for her baby. There was every indication that Krystal would be back.

Krystal promptly left the hospital, catching a taxi with a voucher supplied by the hospital to the Bendigo railway station. Krystal's mother, Karen Fraser, rang her that night from Horsham, where she and her husband operated a mobile wholesale confectionary business. Karen was aware that Krystal had returned to the Bendigo Hospital the previous night and took comfort from the fact that her daughter was there. During the call Karen overheard characteristic background noises suggesting Krystal may have been at a railway station and called her on it.

'You're supposed to be in hospital, what are you doing at the railway station.'

Krystal yelled, 'I'm at the fucking hospital, I'm not at the station, I'm not the only fucking one here you know, there are plenty of others making all the noise here.'

Karen reacted to the hostility and tried to placate her daughter. 'Calm down Belle (the family's nickname for Krystal), I'm sorry, it just sounded like the station.'

Karen was a little shocked at her daughter's volatility over the station observation and assumed she had been wrong. Believing that Krystal was just anxious over the impending birth, she let it go.

Krystal caught the last train home to Pyramid Hill, the 7.42pm. Skinny but for a basketball sized baby bump, 167 centimetres tall, with thick prescription glasses and crooked teeth, Krystal was wearing an orange windcheater, black track pants and a camo baseball cap.

The Melbourne-Swan Hill train was unusually quiet that evening. If it was a normal Saturday night during the football season it would have been full of AFL fans returning home from an afternoon match in Melbourne, but that weekend it was a split round and there was no Saturday game in the city that day. Consequently, there were few passengers on the train as it left Bendigo that evening.

When Krystal got on the train she noticed someone she considered her friend, Hazel Whitmore, an elderly retired businessperson from Boort. The two women knew each other as they were both regular VLine users and Krystal was always up for a chat. The two sat together. On the journey Hazel listened to Krystal describe her excitement about the baby and how she was looking forward to returning to the hospital the following day to deliver her son. Hazel said that Krystal was in good spirits, telling her that she was going to a party in Pyramid Hill that night.

Hazel was worried about how Krystal was going to get back to Bendigo the next day and when Krystal told her that she was going to catch the train back and Hazel had already seen that Krystal's wallet was empty she gave her a $5 note. Believing that was 'a bit stingy' she gave her a second $5 note. She saw Krystal put the money in a plastic bag with a toy from McDonald's. Hazel told me Krystal was her good friend and she missed her dearly.

As Pyramid Hill drew closer, the two women were able to distinguish the familiar powerful spotlight mounted on the abattoirs signifying that they were five minutes from the railway station. The town's famous pyramid shaped hill, a beautiful imposing symbol of strength and security during the day, was invisible at night, disappearing into the

Chapter One   Krystal's final hours

dark countryside. They both left the train at the unmanned Pyramid station upon its arrival there about 8.40 pm.

'Smells like home,' Krystal was overheard saying as she sniffed at the air thick with chimney smoke after leaving the train.

Nick Dingfelder was on the same train that night and as he was preparing to depart at Pyramid Hill he saw Krystal also waiting at the doors to get off and joined her on the platform. A local, Nick new Krystal well. He was returning home to go to a mate's birthday party in town that night. Krystal never mentioned to him that she was also in town for a party. He had questioned Krystal previously about how she'd been able to get her Housing Commission flat. She offered advice and then pulled out some paperwork which she told him would help. Nick described Krystal as being her normal self, happy, as she talked about being induced the next day. They walked along the tracks together for a bit and then Krystal indicated a man walking about five or six metres away from them, who Nick realised had been keeping pace with them. Krystal told Nick that she would have to get going or the bloke would get upset. Krystal veered off and joined the man. He said the guy looked agitated, even embarrassed, "…didn't look like the type of bloke to be hanging around with Krystal, he was well dressed, like he had money, flashy, and her being disabled." He saw Krystal and the man walk off in the direction of the café in Kelly Street.

Nick later described this man to police, a man he had never seen before. In 2022 Nick was shown a photo board containing images of twelve men. He identified one of the men depicted in the images. I have been told that the image selected was not a suspect in Krystal's disappearance. There are rules around how a photo board must be presented. It must contain an image of the suspect and eleven others. The others must be of the same colouring and features as the suspect.

The two staff members working at the Pyramid Hill café remember Krystal entering at about 8.45 pm with an unknown man. One said that Krystal appeared "cranky" with the man. Krystal told them she was going to a party; they were uncertain whether Krystal had said it was at Cohuna or Kerang. They saw the pair leave the shop together and walk in the direction of Krystal's flat a short distance away in Kelly Street. A short time later one of these shop assistants was driving home when she saw Krystal walking alone in the direction of her flat.

It has been established that Krystal arrived at a friend's house in Albert Street, Pyramid Hill, around 9.00 pm. This was the home of Robert Glennie, whose property was located a short distance from Krystal's family home, also in Albert Street. He said Krystal was scared when she arrived at his door, "…banging on the door, she was panicking, like she'd been running."

Glennie said she used his landline to ring Bandy (Alan

Summers) as she'd said she had no credit on her mobile. Glennie said he heard Krystal make arrangements to meet Bandy at the end of Albert Street (intersection with the Pyramid Hill-Bendigo Road) in ten minutes. Telco records indicate that Bandy's mobile was rung seven times from Glennie's phone at this time, none of the calls were answered. Krystal was also apparently annoyed with Jason McPherson, known to Glennie, because he'd failed to fix her computer as he'd promised. She then used Glennie's phone to ring McPherson, who said he apologised to her as he'd forgotten about her computer.

Glennie believed Krystal had actually spoken to Bandy and watched her leave for their "arranged appointment" around 9.30 pm.

Krystal then vanished.

CHAPTER TWO

Missing

Krystal's parents, Karen and Neil, residents of Pyramid Hill for the previous fifteen years, were operating a small business enterprise out of Horsham, selling confectionary throughout the Wimmera and Mallee region from a thirteen-tonne commercial vehicle. They maintained their family home at Pyramid Hill throughout this time and visited there regularly, catching up with Krystal, their son Aaron and Neil's mother Helen, who also lived there. Aaron moved into the family home from the local caravan park with his girlfriend after Karen and Neil rented a property in Horsham to run their business from there.

One week, Karen and Neil would work a three-day week and be home in Pyramid Hill on the Thursday. The subsequent working week involved four days, returning on the Friday to be home every weekend. Karen would spend all day Saturday cooking up meals for Krystal who would turn up with her empty Tupperware containers from the previous week's meals and Karen would fill them up again to get her through the week. Krystal's cooking skills were poor and Karen was determined Krystal's baby would be well nourished through this food she prepared for her.

The Frasers had purchased the Horsham business in 2007, following the sale of the Pyramid Hill bakery café that they had operated for the previous eight years. Scottish born Neil Fraser, forty-nine years old at the time, easygoing but private, a loner in fact, rugged, heavily tattooed with a bikie appearance and hair down to his waist, is best described as a goer. Before the bakery he ran beef cattle on several hundred hectares at Mincha, near Pyramid Hill. Following the loss of the farmhouse in a fire they sold the property and purchased the bakery café. Neil, a qualified plumber, had previously run a large plumbing business contracted to the Ministry of Housing in Melbourne. When he lost this contract, he decided he wanted to be a farmer, moving his parents who had previously farmed in Scotland, on to a second house on the property. Hard working and capable, he had bought the bakery with absolutely no baking experience and through self-tutelage and determination had become a talented baker and pastry chef. Karen Fraser, then forty-seven, a woman of medium height and build, with striking blue eyes and a forthright disposition, had a parallel strong work ethic to that of Neil. She had worked a variety of low-paid jobs, including at Pyramid Salt, "the salt mine," as Pyramid Hill locals colloquially know it. Their then twenty-year-old daughter Chantel accompanied her parents to Horsham and gained employment at a twenty-four-hour Caltex service station, working the graveyard shift. Chantel, a dark haired attractive young woman of medium height with almond shaped eyes and solid build, wears facial piercings and body art. She shared her mother's keen sense of independence, jumping at the chance to leave Pyramid Hill, seeking a change from the strained authenticity of her hometown.

The Fraser's Horsham business was interrupted when Neil was admitted to the Wimmera Base Hospital on 11 June 2009 with acute stomach pain. He was diagnosed as suffering from a severe bout of pancreatitis and a decision was made to remove his gall bladder. The family was acutely aware that Krystal was due to give birth to her son by caesarean at the Bendigo Hospital on Tuesday 23 June 2009. Nevertheless, Karen had been relieved when she learned from Krystal that she had been admitted to the Bendigo Hospital on 15 June to have her baby. Concerned that Krystal had travelled home to Pyramid Hill on Friday 19 June she was again relieved when Krystal rang her late that night and advised her that she had been returned to the Bendigo Hospital by ambulance to have her baby.

Neil was to remain in hospital for a total of ten days and their business was losing money with his extended incapacitation as they were unable to make any sales during the first week of his hospitalisation. Karen estimates they potentially lost $18,000 that first week. Comforted by Krystal's confinement at the Bendigo Hospital and the pace of Neil's recuperation Karen resolved to do the confectionary reveals, she was content that Krystal was in the care of the Bendigo Hospital.

* * *

On Tuesday 23 June 2009, around 11.30 am Karen and Chantel were in the truck doing the sales run when a woman, who identified herself as a midwife from Bendigo Hospital, rang Karen's mobile. Chantel answered it to hear the nurse say, 'Where's Krystal?' Chantel asked the nurse what she meant explaining that Krystal was in their care at the hospital. The midwife told her that Krystal had left the hospital on the Saturday night, discharging herself to attend a party. The nurse asked her to check Krystal's home in an effort to locate her.

Furious at hearing that the hospital had allowed Krystal to leave in the circumstances, Karen rang her mother-in-law, Helen Fraser, in Pyramid Hill and asked her to go around to Krystal's, turning the truck for Pyramid Hill as she spoke. She said to Helen, 'Mum knock on her door, peer through the windows and put your ear up to the door and listen in case she has gone into labour and can't get help.'

Finding no-one at Krystal's Kelly Street flat, Helen rang Karen back and informed her of this. Karen had been trying Krystal's mobile during this time but continued to get the same empty phone company message.

Karen rang the midwife back and advised her of the

failed attempts to locate Krystal and she was told by the staff member, 'We're going to report her missing to police.' Following this, a woman who identified herself as a Department of Human Services (DHS) employee rang Karen and said, 'What kind of mother are you, leaving your heavily pregnant intellectually disabled daughter without support and now she has disappeared?'

Karen said that she told the woman not-too-politely what she could do with her advice. She then inadvertently broke the key off in the ignition of the truck as she was so irritated by this woman and anxious about Krystal. While waiting for a mechanic to repair the ignition, Karen and Chantel rang a variety of people in an effort to locate Krystal. They were becoming frightened for Krystal's wellbeing and baffled by her disappearance. They could not think of any innocuous reason to explain why Krystal was missing but accepted that Krystal would simply get up and go sometimes, visiting friends. Previously though, she always rang Karen to let her know where she was.

Karen said to Chantel, 'It's Tuesday, it took them until today to realise she wasn't there, she was a patient there.'

When Karen and Chantel got to Pyramid Hill about 4.00 pm, they drove directly to the police station to make an official missing person's report in relation to Krystal. Local police officer Senior Constable Jason Brady was on duty but not at the station. They waited a brief time for Brady

Chapter Two Missing

to return, continuing to ring Krystal's mobile which kept repeating the same hollow message.

Conscious of her night blindness, Karen waited for as long as she could before heading to Wedderburn, the next destination on their route, an eighty-kilometre drive, to ensure the truck was off the road before it got dark. With Neil still laid up Karen felt she had to complete the run, had to keep the business going despite her apprehension. Karen said she felt ill with worry on the drive, Krystal's disappearance made no sense at all and she was beginning to think something serious had happened to her daughter.

She planned to make the report at the Wedderburn police station on their arrival. However, she realised that as she didn't know the Wedderburn police officer or have a picture of Krystal and other personal information that the police may require for the report that it would better to make it at Pyramid Hill where Krystal was well known. Consequently, she rang Helen Fraser again and asked her to make the report at Pyramid Hill, which she did that day.

CHAPTER THREE

Initial police response

Movies and television shows have given the general public the impression that a person must be missing for a period; twenty-four hours, two days and so on, before they can be reported as missing. The fact is that a person can be reported missing at any time, there is no time limit to wait. Crime shows have also instilled the appropriate conviction that the early stages of a known or suspected murder are crucial to solving the crime.

The Victoria Police definition of a missing person is:
1. They are reported to police and their whereabouts are unknown; AND
2. There are fears for the safety or concerns for the welfare of that person.

There can be no doubt that the circumstances surrounding Krystal's disappearance met these conditions. While local police conduct initial missing persons investigations, they must be referred to the local Criminal Investigations Unit (CIU), or the homicide squad; depending on the level of risk or suspicious circumstances of the disappearance; in accordance with procedural guidelines in the Victoria Police Manual.

In Australia, there are more than 38,000 missing person reports received every year. While most are found within a brief period, there are currently 2,600 long-term missing persons in the country.

* * *

There were a number of compelling reasons why Senior Constable Jason Brady, the officer initially responsible for the investigation, should have held fears for Krystal's safety and treated her disappearance as a potentially serious crime. These were:

- She had been missing for about sixty hours at the time of reporting.
- Her full-term pregnancy.
- Her enthusiasm to have her baby.
- Her intellectual disability (and consequential vulnerability).
- Recent purchases including a baby stroller, nappies and clothes for the unborn child were still in her flat.
- All her possessions found intact — no missing clothing, bags, cosmetics etc.
- Nothing to indicate she was fabricating her disappearance.
- No resources to fulfill a planned departure — no finances, no vehicle, no benefactor.

- No suggestion that she had been advised by any welfare bodies that she would have to give up her baby (potentially motivating her desire to 'disappear').
- Not answering her mobile — (this would be extremely rare).
- Her self-discharge against staff wishes from maternity accommodation at the Medihotel attached to the Bendigo Hospital to return to Pyramid Hill to attend a party.
- No history of disappearing.
- Never previously reported as a missing person.
- Behaviour out of character.
- No confirmed sightings.
- No contact with her friends or family ('usually rings/texts numerous times a day' - mother).
- Her failure to attend her caesarean appointment at Bendigo Hospital.
- No operation of her bank account.
- No-one emerged as the convener of the party she was attending.
- The person who invited Krystal to the party never surfaced.
- No reasonable explanation for her absence.

These twenty-one condensed points, assessed as an aggregate, demonstrate that Krystal's disappearance represented a probable homicide and should have been treated as such, particularly when there was nothing available to challenge any of these foundations.

Given these compelling grounds the Bendigo CIU, responsible for responding to serious crime in the Pyramid Hill policing area, should have been alerted and responded on the day the report was made, for it is clear that all twenty-one conditions existed at that time. Furthermore, as it would have logically received a copy of the report, it should have acted anyway regardless of whether its support was sought.

Bendigo is eighty-six kilometres south of Pyramid Hill and all Pyramid Hill's neighbouring towns are minor. Leitchville is only slightly larger than Pyramid Hill, with six hundred citizens, Gunbower, has about five hundred and fifty residents, Boort has eight hundred and seventy inhabitants and Cohuna, the largest of its nearest neighbours with a population of two thousand four hundred, is nevertheless a small settlement.

Of these neighbouring communities, there were no police at Leitchville, the nearest community, which was serviced by Mitiamo, a single officer station and sometimes by Cohuna police, where there were only four officers. There is also a single officer situated at Boort. The isolation of Pyramid Hill, in terms of access to police personnel, would clearly have had a bearing on the ability of the local member to investigate serious offences reported in his patch. The fact that it was staffed by a single officer meant that it was even more cogent that the CIU was called to investigate or respond to Krystal's suspicious disappearance. When assistance was required from time to time, the Pyramid Hill police officer could seek assistance from the member stationed at Boort. These members were senior constables, not high-ranking officers and, at the time of Krystal's disappearance, neither had any history or experience in investigating serious crime. The homicide squad, the unit responsible for the investigation of suspected homicides was based in Melbourne, more than two hundred and forty kilometres away.

Major contemporary missing persons cases generated a media frenzy. Notable among them were Karen Ritzevski, the fashion boutique owner who disappeared from her luxury home in middle class Avondale Heights, and Jill Meagher, the beautiful and intelligent twenty-nine-year-old ABC staffer, raped and murdered by recidivist criminal Adrian Bayley while walking to her Brunswick home after having drinks nearby.

Krystal, however, a marginalised and vulnerable young woman given her intellectual disability, and pregnancy without the support of a loving partner, did not receive the same level of amplified attention. The case hardly resonated beyond Pyramid Hill, let alone capturing the hearts and minds of the broader community. Her parents, Karen, and Neil, operating their confectionary business from their Horsham base, were working their arses off, battling to manage debt and facing an increasingly competitive environment amid a shrinking customer base. They were not media savvy and, finding themselves in unfamiliar territory, assumed that the police were doing everything to solve the mystery of their daughter's disappearance. Initially this blind faith was in Sen-Constable Brady.

While I have established that Brady failed to canvass the properties directly across the road from Krystal's flat, which was situated at the front of the block, he did speak to at least one of Krystal's neighbours in the block of fourteen units. That was eighty-eight-year-old Peggy Cameron, who at the time of Krystal's disappearance had lived there for twenty-two years. She said that Krystal visited her on a regular basis and she found her, '...a likeable child-like young girl.' She recently commented that, 'There were people in and out of Krystal's flat for days after her disappearance, no thought of protecting DNA evidence.' It is noteworthy that the protection of a potential crime scene was significant to an elderly woman but possibly not to the investigating officer, who in fairness may not have had any knowledge of these entries. However, it seems pretty clear that the premises were not secured effectively against contamination of and tampering with evidence.

* * *

The Victoria Police Manual reinforces the procedures and guidelines for conducting missing persons investigations, 'In urgent situations where the member believes there is a serious and imminent threat to the life/or health of a person — a member may apply under s.287 of the Commonwealth Telecommunications Act for information held by a telecommunications service provider'[1].

There can be no acceptable reason for this not being undertaken immediately upon receipt of the report given that Krystal had already been missing for almost three days at the time. It should also be asserted that even if Brady didn't believe that Krystal was a missing person the wellbeing of her baby should have focused his thoughts and compelled an urgent response.

While it has been established that phone records from the telco provider of Krystal's mobile hadn't been obtained at the time, the following appeared in the *Bendigo Advertiser* on 13 July 2009, *Leading Senior Constable Jason Brady said Ms Fraser had not used her bank accounts or her mobile phone since disappearing.* However, following this significant discovery, warranting serious concerns for Krystal's welfare, it was followed by the perplexing, *I think she's still alive.*

The public is an absolutely necessary resource in revealing information to assist in an investigation, but when the information the police are sharing with the community is ambiguous or confusing, as was clearly the case here, it is likely to cause the community to believe that Krystal was not a genuine missing person.

Angry and frustrated by Brady's apparent lack of action and initiative, his superficial recognition of Krystal as a missing person and his failure to communicate with them, the Frasers determined to take matters into their own hands. Initially they prepared A4 sized fliers which included Krystal's photo, her description and a brief explanation of her disappearance. These were distributed throughout the Loddon shire by family and friends. Following this, Krystal's sister Chantel set up a public Facebook group titled, 'Help us find Krystal Fraser.'

While this networking group generated an abundance of information, none of it proved effective in resolving this mystery. Of the numerous posts there have been around two hundred people who identified themselves as a 'dear friend,' 'great friend,' 'mate' and simply 'friend' of Krystal; in life, however, Krystal never experienced such recognition or affection. At times, the monitoring and managing of the website became a real imposition for Karen and Chantel. Along with the countless sympathies and good wishes there was the occasional false hope, criticism, invention, insult and ridicule. At the time of writing there are 2300 members of this group.

CHAPTER FOUR

Role of Senior Constable Jason Brady

Jason Brady transferred from the busy outer metropolitan police station of Melton to Pyramid Hill in 2008. At that time, he had sixteen years policing experience, all in uniform operational duties in the busy western suburbs of Melbourne, patrolling in a police vehicle and responding to calls in a reactive role. Having had this number of years in policing and to be still at the rank of sen-constable suggested he either wasn't interested in or was considered unsuitable for promotion to the rank of sergeant.

Pyramid Hill was one of a slightly more than a hundred single officer police stations operating in the state at that time, referred to then in police vernacular as 'one-manners.' However, with women being integrated into more policing roles and to help overcome the negative aspects of policing language and culture, they are now officially referred to as one-person stations and at the time of writing two of these roles are occupied by women. Police attached to these single member stations are judged by their communities as individuals first and subsequently as coppers. Keeping your own house in order, not sharing secrets obtained on the job, not getting drunk at the pub but turning up at the pub, showing a real interest in the town and its people, and the old police maxim of "keeping your dick in your pants" have always been the fundamental criteria for acceptance.

Jason Brady, short and stocky, had been labelled "puffer fish" by some locals because of his stance of standing with shoulders pulled back and chest pushed out. He was perceived locally by some as a heavy drinker, spending too much time at the pub, a gossip, and far too regularly in and out of personal relationships. Living in a fishbowl subjects a person to immense public scrutiny and reputations; good and bad, are quickly established in tiny rural towns like Pyramid Hill. Brady did have his supporters but they have been less vocal.

Brady was responsible for taking and submitting the missing person's report for Krystal made by her paternal grandmother Helen Fraser to him at Pyramid Hill on the afternoon of Tuesday 23 June 2009. Helen, seventy-two at the time, fit, healthy and alert, had last seen Krystal when she picked her up from the Pyramid Hill railway station about 11.40 am on Friday 19 June 2009. Surprised that Krystal was able to leave the hospital after her admission earlier that week Helen said she felt she was "up to something" because she wouldn't explain why she had checked herself out to return home. She recalled that, *Krystal was acting like she did when she had done something or was lying about something.*

Helen said Brady was dismissive of her when taking

the report, suggesting that Krystal had made her way to Horsham to see her dad as he had been made aware that Neil was in hospital there. She said Brady never provided her with a copy of the missing person's report, as required. Helen alleged that when she hadn't heard back from Brady a couple of weeks later, she rang him and ...*he just wiped me, said Krystal was just hiding out.* Other than a request from the police media unit for a photo of Krystal, Helen said she has never been contacted by another police officer, despite making the report herself.

The first public notification of Krystal's status as a missing person appeared on the website of the *Bendigo Advertiser* at 4.09 pm on the day following the report, Wednesday 24 June 2009. It stated that Krystal was last seen within the maternity accommodation section of the Bendigo Hospital at 6.30 pm on Saturday 20 June 2009. Media coverage continued to report that the last sighting of Krystal was at this location, "She was last seen at the maternity accommodation section of the Bendigo Hospital..." (*Bendigo Advertiser* website accessed 9.38 am 21 July 2009). Unquestionably, police would have established by this stage that Krystal had caught the 7.42 pm train from Bendigo to Pyramid Hill following her departure from the hospital. The purpose of the police using the media in these circumstances would clearly have been aimed at engaging the public in solving the mystery. By continuing to allow the publication of inaccurate information an opportunity may have been missed. Brady was continually quoted in posts and publications alongside this information and the error should have been obvious to him and consequently rectified by him or other police officers involved in or overseeing the investigation.

When I tracked down Jason Brady he was working as a ranger at a regional city council and is no longer a member of Victoria Police. He initially showed a strong reluctance to answer questions about his role in Krystal's investigation but when told the family held him responsible for its failure he asked me to send through a list of questions which he would address.

I emailed him a document containing a hundred and forty-three questions but received no response. I had figured that I might only get the one opportunity so had been determined to cover as much ground as possible but realised in hindsight that this had been a mistake. The quantity and gravity of the questions possibly panicked him. I rang him again and he did respond to a number of questions. He acknowledged that he had become aware that Krystal had caught the Saturday evening train from Bendigo to Pyramid Hill the day after he took the missing person's report but did not offer any explanation for the persistent media error, namely, that she was last seen in Bendigo.

On the question of the nature of his relationship with Krystal he said, 'I kept an eye out for her, most of the town did, she was my friend. I tried to help her, got her involved with psyches from Echuca. I knew she was using a lot of dope but was not aware of her association with so many blokes until after the details of her phone contacts were obtained.'

Asked what action he took after the receipt of the missing person report from Helen Fraser, he said, 'I spoke to my inspector and informed the CIU that day. I also made contact with the Bendigo Hospital and travelled there the following morning. There I spoke to management and viewed CCTV footage.'

When I asked him if he inspected Krystal's possessions at the hospital, he offered, 'There was only a few bits of clothing, nothing was seized.' Asked if he saw Krystal's diary among her belongings, he said, 'No, I think one was seized from her flat, the homicide squad took it, it just had stuff in it about the baby.'

Krystal's diary was recovered from the hospital by homicide officers after they became involved. Krystal's entries in her diary, made while there in the last week of her life, offer an insight into a person later suspected of having been responsible for her disappearance and death. More on this later.

Karen advises that following an appeal to Brady, he, with the help of his close friend, local CFA member Mark Lacey, forced entry to Krystal's flat via a flywire screen the week of the report of her disappearance. Karen had tasked Brady with looking for any signs to indicate whether Krystal might have returned. Karen said that Brady told her that the premises

Chapter Four Role of Senior Constable Jason Brady

appeared intact, reporting that there was no sign of a struggle but there was also no sign of Krystal. According to Mark Lacey they didn't search the place, as they simply wanted to see if there was any indication that Krystal may have been there or something to indicate where she might have gone. He said he observed a new stroller, baby clothes and other items for the newborn in the flat. He further revealed that nothing was seized from the premises by Brady, except for a spare set of keys located on a keyboard. He said that Brady used these keys to secure the premises on their departure. Speaking to Brady about this search I asked him if there was anything discovered in Krystal's flat that led him to believe that she had packed a bag or two and simply gone into hiding of her own accord. He said there wasn't.

Karen advised me that Neil, Chantel and she returned to Pyramid Hill following Neil's release from hospital the end of that first week after Krystal's disappearance. Karen said she went to see Brady at the police station and said to him, 'There is no way my girl has just taken off somewhere, she is not hiding out somewhere. She is not capable of hiding; she has been the victim of a crime. Do you understand that?'

She said Brady replied with, 'Well that's what people are telling me, she is always just jumping on the train and shooting off somewhere.'

Karen said she told Brady, 'But she comes shooting back just as quickly and when and wherever she does go she rings or texts me to let me know, her phone is turned off for the first time in her life, you must appreciate this is different, she was supposed to have had her baby by now. Please do something.'

Karen said she asked Brady to track Krystal through her Medicare card to see if she was in hospital somewhere. She also requested approval to go to Krystal's flat; the family had already been told by Helen Fraser that Brady had told her 'in no uncertain terms' to tell them to stay out of the way and to not go anywhere near Krystal's flat. Brady is said to have refused the request, telling Karen that the flat was being secured as Krystal was a missing person and no-one was allowed in.

At this time none of the Fraser family, including Helen who had triggered the report, had been contacted by Brady or any other police with any updates. Karen said she also asked Brady if he had been in contact with the Bendigo Hospital and he told her that he had and there was nothing to report from there.

As mentioned previously, this commentary comes into dispute later on when the homicide squad recovered Krystal's diary from there. Asked if she knew what avenues of inquiry Brady had been pursuing, Karen said, 'He was doing fuck all I reckon, but he'd shut me completely out, never a phone call, so I just don't know.'

Karen said she was concerned that Brady was not communicating with the family at all and disturbed that he was continuing to openly state in the media that Krystal was simply hiding out, with the following quote attributed to him in the *Bendigo Advertiser* of 3 July 2009, *...believes she may have gone underground...Krystal may be scared to come forward...believed she was hiding out in the Bendigo area.* And again, on 13 July with, *I think she's still alive, she's relatively street wise and I've got a gut feeling.* Which was followed on 21 July by, *Sen-Constable Brady believes Krystal may have fled interstate as she had concerns the state would take her son after his birth.*

Given the frequency and continuity of these remarks from Brady it is reasonable to assume that he was not considering that Krystal may have been the victim of a crime but rather a runaway. Later observations and speculation led some malevolent locals to suggest that Brady may have been comfortable with the fact that Krystal had disappeared. This may have been as a result of unfair and unfounded gossip surrounding a potential sexual relationship between Brady and Krystal.

Karen said she could not understand why Brady continued to suggest that Krystal was simply hiding out as there was simply nothing to support this assertion. She had told Brady early in the enquiry that Krystal had been a participant at a meeting with Department of Health and Human Services (DHHS) personnel and Karen at which it was agreed that Krystal could keep her baby. A contingency had also been developed at this meeting for Karen to assist if and where necessary in the care of the baby and assume foster care if deemed unavoidable

Karen said that when she later raised Brady's public statements asserting that Krystal was simply hiding out with him that he told her, '...because you got DHS involved and they were gonna take the baby, that's why she ran away.' Karen said she told him this was not going to happen as 'Krystal knew that she was allowed to keep her baby and DHS left her in no doubt of that. She also knew that I would never ever have let anybody take that baby.'

I raised this with Brady and he offered, 'I was aware that DHS was involved and Krystal had been told by them that they were going to take the baby. I was trying to appease the family by saying she was in hiding.'

I asked him if he'd had this conversation with Karen Fraser and he said, 'Karen just didn't believe it.' Questioned as to his source he told me that he was briefed at the Bendigo Hospital when he made enquiries there the day after taking the missing person report. However, in a follow up conversation, Brady was far more definitive in this regard suggesting that he had been made aware by DHS before the birth and that both Karen and Krystal were in no doubt that DHS was going to take the baby as Krystal had been assessed as unfit to keep the baby, adding that, 'Krystal was even telling people in town this.'

During the course of my research and countless interviews for this book this possibility was never raised by anyone who knew Krystal. Basically, everyone who had discussed the impending birth with her described Krystal as enthusiastic and excited about it. Indeed, Hazel Whitmore, who sat next to Krystal on the train journey from Bendigo to Pyramid Hill on the night of Krystal's subsequent disappearance, and possibly the last person ever to speak to Krystal about her baby, described Krystal's passion and animation at the imminent arrival of her baby. The prospect of the removal of her baby clearly appears not to have been contemplated by Krystal.

As a result of Brady's comments, it became imperative that I obtain any correspondence held by the DHS relating to Krystal's case. Karen Fraser tried to gain access to Krystal's file and was told there was no longer any documentation held on her daughter. My mate and former police colleague Bob Kerr was able to successfully track down the former DHS child protection officer who was the case worker in Krystal's pregnancy. She was no longer employed by the organisation but spoke to Bob on the condition of anonymity, although she had previously made a statement to homicide investigators. Bob said that she had instant recall of Krystal's case, telling him that she still experienced nausea whenever there was media coverage of Krystal's disappearance.

She told Bob that she met Krystal in her official capacity on a number of occasions and described her as a 'lovely girl'. She said that she felt she had gained Krystal's trust during their dealings. She said that their final interaction was at a pre-birth meeting at Karen's house in Pyramid Hill, which took place close to Krystal's admission to hospital for the birth. She remembered that those present at this meeting were:

1. Child protection officer (DHS),
2. Maternity support worker (Bendigo Health),
3. Early childhood worker (PASDS),
4. Karen Fraser,
5. Krystal Fraser.

She said the purpose of the meeting was to determine and establish what action would be taken and what services would need to become involved after the birth. It was agreed that the hospital would prepare a report after the child was born and following a five-day course at St Luke's Bendigo (Anglicare Victoria) where Krystal would be taught mothering skills, during which the child protection officer would monitor her progress. The child protection officer said the fact that there was a case worker from the Parenting Assessment and Skills Development Service (PASDS) suggested that a twelve-week home based development course was also planned for Krystal and her child. The program involved twenty visits of two hours duration by an early childhood worker to a new mother's home during the first twelve weeks of the child's life, where parenting skills would be taught and assessed.

Cleary the monitoring of Krystal and her baby was planned to continue after the child's birth. The child protection worker told Bob, '...there was never any discussion or decision about taking the baby, in fact there was never any suggestion that DHS would remove the baby either during our meetings with the family or internally at child protection. Krystal understood that we planned to visit her and the baby in hospital, talk to her, offer support, and work out how we were going to proceed after they left St Luke's.'

When Bob advised her of what Brady had said about the removal of Krystal's child, she said that police were never involved at any stage during Krystal's pregnancy. She added that she did not know Brady and had never spoken to him or any other police until after Krystal's disappearance, when a uniform police officer from Bendigo questioned her about Krystal.

She said that she told this officer the facts as described above. The only other recollection she had of police at the time was overhearing a comment at her office that a police officer (unknown) was saying that it was all child protection's fault because they had told Krystal they were removing the child.

The child protection officer insisted that this was plainly wrong. A decision of this type had not been made in any regard and, more importantly, the DHS agency, '...never ever disclosed that a child would be taken prior to the birth as a precaution against the parent/s taking off with the child.'

It appears evident that Brady's mistaken belief that DHS had planned to remove Krystal's baby and, more critically, that Krystal had been made aware of this fallacy had shaped his initial unproductive investigation. It is possible that Brady became aware that DHS was involved in the case early on in his investigation and formed the questionable view that Krystal's baby was going to be removed following the birth as a consequence of the agency's involvement, without ascertaining the true facts. An inaccurate opinion that he undoubtedly shared with other police personnel which he continued to indicate on a regular basis with the media, including up until 10 August 2009, fifty-one days after the last known sighting of Krystal.

It seems obvious that Brady failed to evaluate his theory for Krystal's disappearance, which that's all it could have ever been, by making enquiries with the Department of Human Services.

It is worth revisiting the initial comments attributed to Brady by Helen Fraser when she made the missing report to him, with him telling her that Krystal had probably made her way to Horsham to visit her father in hospital there. There was no mention of DHS involvement at that time.

Brady acknowledged that Krystal had never been reported as a missing person previously. Asked what other enquiries he made in an effort to locate Krystal, he said, 'I contacted bus companies, made enquiries at the railway station, arranged for footage (CCTV) at Bendigo railway station and contacted hospitals in the region.' His canvass of Krystal's neighbours has already been addressed, where it is alleged that he failed to speak to those living directly across the road from the block of units and who had an uninterrupted view of Krystal's unit at the front of the block and adjacent to the road.

Chapter Four   Role of Senior Constable Jason Brady

* * *

I met Debbie Demaine, the former joint publican of the Victoria Hotel in Pyramid Hill, at Karen Fraser's house during my first sanctioned interview with Karen. Debbie had operated the town's only pub with her husband David for more than twelve years between 2008 and 2020. She had watched Krystal grow up and when Krystal started coming to the pub, kept a lookout for her.

She said Brady first went into the pub asking questions about Krystal six weeks after her disappearance. She told me she said to him, 'Jason, it has been six weeks, we are six weeks down the track, I can't remember every little detail of what happened six weeks ago. An awful lot happens in a pub over that length of time.' She said Brady only asked her about the last time she had seen Krystal in the pub. 'He then moved on to someone else at the bar and I felt that it was almost as if he wasn't treating the matter seriously. He was sort of mocking Krystal as he spoke to patrons. He wasn't even asking questions; he was simply discussing her disappearance.'

Debbie recalled that Brady attended at the pub the following two Sundays after this, adding that he was quite drunk on both occasions. In the first episode, she said he went along everyone at the bar, 'Mouthing off about Kaz (Karen Fraser) and Neil. I didn't hear it all, he was just criticising them, then he came to me and I told him he was talking to the wrong person. The next week he came in and it was obvious he had had a lot to drink. Again he approached everyone at the bar telling them that there was going to be search for Krystal of the Common, the following day. He approached me and told me the same story, I asked him if the family knew and he said no, I told him that they should be the ones he's telling, not the whole pub.'

Brady's apparent lack of professionalism does not conceal or moderate his failure to conduct an appropriate unbiased investigation into Krystal's disappearance. With Victoria Police being a rigid hierarchical structure, Brady's immediate supervising officer was the sergeant in charge of Wedderburn police station, fifty-six kilometres to the southwest of Pyramid Hill. It would have been this officer's role to debrief Brady on his investigation and determine if any further enquiries should be made or additional resources were required. It is reasonable to assume that in discussions with this supervising officer Brady advanced the same theory he had adopted throughout, namely, that Krystal was simply hiding out and not at risk.

Karen Fraser recalled that Brady told her about a month into the enquiry, '...my boss from Wedderburn told me that I've had the file for too long, time to drop it.' Karen said she couldn't help feeling that Brady said this in a way to imply that his boss had implied, 'she's only a nuffer after all.' But she thinks that this was more about Brady's bias than his supervisor's, or a reflection of the tension between them.

It should be remembered that at this stage of the enquiry

Karen was incredibly angry with Brady and the quality of his investigation into Krystal's disappearance. There was also some alleged history between the Fraser family and Brady. During a conversation with Helen Fraser at her home in October 2020, she told me that she was at the local bowls club before Krystal's disappearance, where Brady was talking to a group of about four bowlers, including herself. She said he began criticising Krystal, allegedly telling the group that he had a large folder of information about her and what a nuisance she was.

Helen said one of the group said to Brady, 'Oh Jason, have you met Helen?' The introduction was effected and the person then said, 'Helen is Krystal's grandmother.' Brady apparently left quickly as a result. On the occasion of Krystal's twenty-first birthday party, held at the local pub, the family were surprised to see Brady in attendance but accepted that as Krystal had invited him, he was welcome. However, both Neil and his son Aaron Fraser have said that Brady approached them separately during the party asking them to 'sort a bloke out,' referring to a young bloke allegedly dealing dope out of the local caravan park. They have said that while Brady was 'pissed' what he was asking them to do was 'dodgy.' Brady denied these allegations.

Irrespective of what Brady was telling his superior at Wedderburn, that police officer, along with detectives at Bendigo CIU, should have assumed that Krystal was in danger/at risk until the facts proved otherwise. A missing person enquiry draws a unique burden compared to other investigations. For instance, if police are presented with a body, their first consideration is whether a crime has been committed. There are a number of options for investigators to consider: Is the death a consequence of natural causes, accident, suicide, self-defence or murder?

In the case of a missing person, however, investigators must assume that a crime has been committed from the outset when there is no evidence to the contrary. This does not seem to have been the process in Krystal's case.

I am told that Brady was moved out of his role in charge of the Pyramid Hill police station early in 2010 to work at a number of larger stations in the region for his wellbeing. He later returned to his previous role at Pyramid Hill for a brief time before taking extended sick leave, eventually being officially discharged from Victoria Police following a diagnosis of post-traumatic stress disorder. He remains on a police pension for life.

Of interest to me was what he might have recorded in the missing person report about the circumstances of Krystal's disappearance. When I asked him, he said, 'You just record the facts, as you know them.' I then asked if there was an opportunity to record his thoughts or opinions based on his own knowledge of Krystal and her habits in the report and he said, 'No, nothing like that.' I immediately thought this was bullshit although it had been an exceptionally long time since I'd seen a Victoria Police missing person report.

I then spoke to a couple of serving members and established, as I recalled, that there is and was then, a narrative section in the report where a member is encouraged to provide information known to them that may assist other officers to locate the subject of the report. For example, if a member suspected that a reported missing person was in hiding for a particular reason and not genuinely missing or was a frequently reported missing person it is plausible that this would be shared with others.

Brady also made the following comment during this discussion, 'If the family want to blame someone because there has never been an arrest then they can blame me but to say I wasn't taking the matter seriously or doing my best then that is absolute bullshit. I don't believe I could have done anymore. Before they start pointing the finger at me maybe they should have a look in their own backyard. They took off to Horsham and left that poor kid to her own devices and they didn't give a fuck, and this led to her downfall.'

He added that his retirement from Victoria Police as a consequence of a diagnosis of post-traumatic stress disorder was due to his inability to solve Krystal's disappearance.

While I have been critical of Brady's inflexible belief that Krystal had orchestrated her own disappearance and was not a genuine missing person, a belief that thwarted a timely and thorough criminal investigation, he did try to locate Krystal and her baby. DetSgt Wayne Woltsche of the homicide squad, who was to lead the investigation later, has said that Brady,

'Did all the right things, identified and had spoken to all the right people, but his investigation was based on Krystal turning up alive.'

Woltsche had no doubt that Brady believed Krystal was going to turn up. He also thought, 'police further down the track' were of the same opinion, including those further up the line, superiors Brady had briefed. These included Det-SenConstable Mark Crossley of Bendigo CIU, who initially believed Brady's endeavours were to find her but soon concluded something had happened to her.

Woltsche went on to say that Brady was inexperienced in an investigation of this type and had all the responsibilities and duties of a single officer police station to deal with, normal day to day routine activities. I mentioned Brady's failure to seek Krystal's telephone records. However, according to Woltsche, he did make a request to Krystal's telco provider to locate Krystal's mobile by using 'triangulation.' Police still use this terminology but the expression relates to a system that was used before mobile phones became GPS enabled. Because a mobile phone usually communicates with three towers at any one time, the strength of the signal, and the time it takes for the signal to reach each of the towers, can be used to provide an approximate location for the mobile using the triangulation method. Since mobile phones have become GPS supported the telco operator will 'ping' the phone by sending a message to the phone number and the automatic response from the phone will provide a reasonably accurate latitude and longitude determined by GPS[2].

For either system to work the mobile phone must have power, it must be turned on. Krystal's phone was turned off at 2.49 am on 21 June 2009, thus preventing this process.

CHAPTER FIVE

Preservation of the Scene

Karen Fraser said that the first time she and Neil were permitted to enter Krystal's flat was at the end of the first or second week after Krystal's disappearance. She said Brady met them there and let them in using a spare key he said he had removed from Krystal's flat upon his initial entry with Mark Lacey. The single key, Karen recalled, was for the front security door and when Brady unlocked it he simply opened the front timber door which was unlocked, there was no key for it.

Karen said she noted that the back door and its security door were snibbed from the inside. As far as she was concerned this was a cursory search to help them determine if Krystal may have returned at some point or if there was something to indicate where she may have gone. Karen said she and Neil were both rocked at the spectacle of all the baby stuff, things that she knew a newborn baby would have needed. She said they quickly left the flat in the belief that Krystal had experienced something potentially tragic based on what they had seen.

Chapter Five Preservation of the Scene

Karen said that shortly after Krystal's disappearance Sue Lacey, A family friend who had taken Krystal to see doctors in Boort during her pregnancy, texted her and asked her if she would mind if she and Rebecca Fossett, another friend, cleaned Krystal's flat and washed her clothes.

Karen said she told her, 'Yes I do. If anybody's going to clean it, it ought to be me.' She said she didn't want anybody else rifling through her daughter's personal stuff and told Sue, 'But you can't anyway because no-one is allowed in the place, Brady told us that.'

Karen said Sue said she would go to see Jason (Brady) about it. Karen said she repeated that no-one was allowed in because Krystal was a missing person. She said Sue rang her back a short time later telling her that Jason had given them the OK.

Karen said she was exasperated by this; the family weren't allowed in but these two women who were not family were. She told me she said to Sue something like, 'Of course, you're Sue Lacey, I'm only her mother.' Karen said that she learnt from Sue that they had found a green canvas supermarket bag on the couch at Krystal's flat and in it was Krystal's wallet containing her bank and Medicare cards. Karen said Sue told her that they had 'shit themselves' and contacted Brady who told them to get out of there. Sue was married to Mark Lacey at the time. Both were friends of Brady.

At the time I raised the visit to Krystal's flat with Sue, she didn't recall removing anything from the flat, saying that they left in a hurry after discovering Krystal's wallet. I have also spoken to Rebecca who, like Sue, has also left Pyramid Hill. She said she was very reluctant to enter Krystal's flat but Sue assured her that they had approval to clean the premises.

She said the flat was a mess, with clothes strewn across the floor and dirty dishes in the sink. She found Krystal's wallet and said she instantly understood the ominous meaning of it. Sue rang Brady and they immediately left. She said that all she took from the flat was Krystal's goldfish which she took home and kept for many years afterwards, her children naming the fish 'Krystal.' She acknowledged that entry was gained via a window as they did not have a key and that it was the second weekend after Krystal's disappearance. She said that it had been her intention to clean out Krystal's fridge and remove any rubbish.

I have difficulty understanding why Brady didn't appreciate the significance of the discovery of Krystal's wallet by Sue and Rebecca. Sue determined that the find took place on 30 June 2009, ten days after Krystal's disappearance, which coincides with Rebecca's recollection of the timing. Krystal's disappearance up until that point had been widely regarded, because of media reporting of Brady's perspective, as a simple runaway.

However, despite the discovery of the wallet and its disturbing implications, Brady continued being quoted in the media on 3, 13, 21 and 27 July, communicating that Krystal was simply 'hiding out'; with a final reference on 10 August where he was quoted publicly again declaring that she was hiding out in New South Wales with her baby.

Did finding the wallet not suit the scenario that Brady had fashioned, therefore leading him to ignore its potential relevance? If the discovery of the wallet alone did not cause foreboding over Krystal's disappearance, the fact that all her recent purchases for the baby were still in her flat should have aroused serious concerns for her welfare. It was blatantly obvious to Sue and Rebecca that Krystal's wallet being in the flat was alarming, having 'shit themselves' and quickly fled the flat. It appears that this highly relevant discovery was not shared with other police; if it had been surely alarm bells would have immediately sounded.

On another occasion, following concerns raised by Karen and Chantel that the photograph of Krystal used in media reporting of her disappearance was some years old, Brady asked Karen to provide him with a recent photo of Krystal. They were still living in Horsham and all their possessions had been warehoused in one room of the Pyramid Hill house. Karen said she mentioned this to Brady, saying that she wouldn't know where to look for a photo there but knew there were recent photos of Krystal in her album at the flat. Karen said she told him, 'You've got the keys to Krystal's flat; I'll meet you there and get one out of Krystal's album.' She recalls that Brady told her he had already looked and couldn't find the album. Karen said they agreed to meet at Krystal's flat at a given time to locate the photo album.

She said she had been waiting for Brady outside Krystal's flat for about an hour when Sue Lacey appeared and asked what she was doing. Karen said she told her she was waiting there to meet Brady to find a photograph of Krystal for the media. Karen said Sue told her that she had just provided Brady with a photo taken at Krystal's twenty-first birthday. Karen said she drove straight to the police station and confronted Brady, recalling, 'Brady came out to the counter all smiles and I said to him, you're not a copper's arsehole you fuckin' wanker, how dare you leave me waiting for an hour when you've already had Sue pick up a photo?'

Karen said she was livid and when Brady picked up his cap and began to walk past her out of the station she said to him, 'You don't do that, ask for something, agree to meet and then get someone else to get it and then not turn up to tell me.'

Karen said that later in 2009, after the homicide squad had become involved and within a couple of weeks of Chantel's twenty-first birthday (7 October), she contacted Brady and arranged to collect keys to Krystal's flat for the purpose of cleaning it. Karen said that it was evident to her by this stage that Krystal would never be returning, and the flat had been forensically examined and cleared for handover to the family.

Karen said when she arrived at the police station with Chantel, Brady handed her a new set of keys saying that he had to change the locks to secure the premises properly. He told them he had got Helen Fraser to sign a form allowing this to happen. Karen said she asked him where Krystal's key was and Brady said because he had to secure the place, he had had to get new locks installed. Karen said she reminded him that he had Krystal's key to lock the place up but he denied he had ever had possession of Krystal's key. Karen couldn't understand why he said this because he had clearly used it to gain entry with her and Neil earlier on. She said Chantel began to question Brady about this, but she nudged her with her foot to remain silent. She said she didn't push it because she felt it was better to keep him onside, aware that their relationship had been caustic throughout the investigation.

Karen said that they collected the new keys to Krystal's flat from Brady on a Saturday. On arrival at the flat she was shocked to see that vomit that had been on the toilet floor had been cleaned up, Krystal's bed had been made and had fresh linen on it. It had been dirty when Neil and Karen first visited with Brady. She said all Krystal's clothes, which had been dirty and tossed all over the floor of the bedroom, had been washed and placed in drawers as well. She assumed Sue Lacey and Rebecca Fossett must have done all this back in June before the forensic testing of Krystal's flat and said she felt that any DNA evidence would have been lost in the process.

Sue Lacey and Rebecca Fossett initially denied washing Krystal's bedding and clothing when I spoke to them. However, Sue recently responded to a query from Chantel and acknowledged that she believed she did in fact wash the clothing and bedding in Krystal's flat. She told Chantel that they entered Krystal's flat on 30 June 2009 and washed the clothing and bedding during the first week of July (2009). This clearly charitable exercise in support of the Fraser family just may well have worked in the interests of the offender as it was all accomplished before police had begun treating Krystal's disappearance as a crime.

There had obviously been an entry to Krystal's flat to recover these items and a subsequent one to return them, further contaminating a possible crime scene. Not to mention the destruction of any evidence on the bedding or clothing.

* * *

Karen and Chantel were both aware that Krystal had obtained a geneticist's report following her admission to Mercy Women's Hospital in Heidelberg in May 2009, a precaution given Krystal's hydrocephalus. Chantel said that she had last seen the report on the desk next to Krystal's computer but despite a thorough search of the entire flat they could not locate it. They both understood that the test may have yielded a DNA profile of the baby's father, irrefutable proof of paternity.

Its absence is potentially significant. Having completed the housekeeping, they locked the flat again with the keys provided and retained them, as arranged with Brady. They returned the next day to collect the mop and bucket, Karen remaining in the car out the front while Chantel entered the flat to retrieve the cleaning equipment.

Chapter Five Preservation of the Scene

Chantel said she almost tripped over Krystal's photo album which was on the floor just inside the front door and at the same time heard someone running out the back door of Krystal's flat. She said her view of the back door was obscured by the loungeroom/kitchen wall facing the front door. Chantel said she rushed towards the back door and all she saw was the security door swinging in the breeze. She swore they had locked both back doors when they left the previous day, but they could be unlocked internally without a key.

Chantel said she ran out to Karen and asked her if she had seen someone running from the flat. She hadn't but there were two routes from the flat, out the front to Kelly Street or down the back towards the other flats in the complex and the railway line directly behind. Despite a search of the area no-one was detected.

Chantel said they entered the flat together and looked through the photo album, which they agreed had been on Krystal's bed when they left the previous afternoon. there was a photo missing from the book, it was above one of Brady, Krystal and another male taken at Krystal's twenty-first. Brady had his arm around Krystal in the photo. Chantel remembers seeing the missing photo previously and it was of Krystal and a man unknown to her. The two women say that they also observed that books and paperwork that had been stacked up at the back door on the Friday had been moved away from the doorway.

One of the most important aspects of evidence preservation and collection is protecting the crime scene. It doesn't appear that any effective measures were taken to secure and protect Krystal's flat from contamination or even worse from evidence tampering.

In saying that, Brady had the opportunity when he first entered the flat with CFA officer Mark Lacey to determine if a crime may have been committed by effecting a disciplined and methodical examination of the flat. It is conceivable that he would have changed his subjective outlook of believing that Krystal was simply 'hiding out' to the more enlightened assessment that she was indeed a victim if he'd located the wallet and its contents. The distinctive police crime tape that was widely used and available at the time was not used.

As chronicled, in addition to Brady and Mark Lacey's initial entry and the 'appraisal' entry by Karen and Neil with Brady, there appear to have been further entries conceivably 'authorised' by Brady before the forensic examination by crime scene officers. There was one by Sue Lacey to clean Krystal's flat, where the wallet was found, the further entry, only recently acknowledged by her to collect clothing and bedding, and the subsequent return of these laundered items. The latter entries were apparently conducted in Brady's absence despite his warnings to the Fraser family that no-one was permitted to enter.

It is feasible that Brady had also entered on another occasion looking for a recent photo of Krystal, given the

Chapter Five   Preservation of the Scene

comment made to Karen Fraser about not being able to locate Krystal's photo album. It is also worth recalling Krystal's elderly neighbour, Peggy Cameron's comment, 'There were people in and out for days after her disappearance, not a thought of protecting DNA.'

When asked recently about the keys to Krystal's flat and entries to it, Brady said, 'I always attended her flat with Dale Lewis, the member (police officer) from Serpentine and a member of the Fraser family. I never went there alone to ensure the preservation of evidence and I didn't allow anyone else to go there for the same reason. The Frasers had a key and they would open the door to the flat and lock it when we left. They eventually provided me with a set of the keys.'

When advised of other known visits to the flat he said, 'I was not aware of any other visits, there were none authorised by me.'

CHAPTER SIX

Criminal Investigation Unit Involvement

Forty-nine days after Krystal's last sighting, and forty-six days subsequent to the missing person report, the participation of the Bendigo CIU was revealed for the first time in a post on the *Bendigo Advertiser's* website at 9.14 am on 8 August 2009. Det-Sen-Constable Mark Crossley was quoted, 'Police still hold grave fears for the safety of Krystal and her baby.' It could be reasoned that these grave fears had failed to surface before this. What changed in the investigation that led to this newfound clarity?

From the information available, it appears that Krystal's disappearance did not become significant to police until details of calls to and from her mobile phone became available. Analysis of these calls, known as CCRs (call charge records) in police parlance, obviously put an end to speculation that she was simply in hiding. If Krystal's disappearance had been treated as potentially life-threatening from the outset these phone records would have been obtained promptly as stated previously.

Chapter Six   Criminal Investigation Unit Involvement

The information obtained from Krystal's mobile telecommunications provider showed that there were nineteen calls made from the phone box outside the Leitchville post office to Krystal over a period of about five weeks before her disappearance. There had never been calls to her mobile from this phone box before 14 May 2009, the day the calls to Krystal commenced.

Of interest to investigators was the fact that the telco records showed there had been frequent phone calls between Krystal and a Peter Jenkinson of Gunbower over an extended period, but these had ceased on 13 May 2009. This final call lasted nine and a half minutes.

Of greater interest still was the revelation that there were two calls to Krystal's mobile from this phone box on the day of her disappearance, Saturday 20 June 2009. A call received late in the afternoon is suspected of having been the cause of Krystal's untimely departure from the maternity accommodation wing of the Bendigo Base Hospital; possibly an invitation to a party to be held that night. Staff at the hospital had urged Krystal not to leave as she was due to have her baby and had been conveyed to the facility by ambulance when experiencing contractions earlier that day. Despite their efforts, she left after assuring staff that she would return the next morning. Following her return to Pyramid Hill, Krystal received the second of the calls from the same phone box at 11.59 pm. This caller appears to have been the last person to have spoken to Krystal before her disappearance. It was indeed the last call she ever received on her mobile.

The telco information also disclosed that another two calls were made to Krystal's mobile from the phone box on the previous day, Friday 19 June 2009, one while she was still at the hospital and another later that day after she had returned to Pyramid Hill. There was also a call from the phone box to Krystal's mobile on the Tuesday of that week, following Krystal's initial admission. The significance of this call is discussed at length later when person of interest Peter Jenkinson is scrutinised.

It is not known if the public phone box was forensically examined but neighbouring properties were canvassed for potential witnesses to identify the mystery caller who had been ringing Krystal. According to Leitchville locals I spoke to, this canvass was conducted by uniform personnel from Cohuna police station, not by detectives.

It should be noted that at the time of Krystal's disappearance the Leitchville post office, was located in a residential street and not in the town's shopping precinct. Essentially, it was out of the way, hidden in the back streets.

The earliest reference to the Bendigo CIU is in the *Bendigo Advertiser* where it is reported that, 'One lead police have is a phone call,' and Detective Senior Constable Crossley is quoted, 'We need that person to contact us and provide any information they might have.'

Importantly, investigators have confirmed that there was

never another call from that phone box to Krystal's mobile after the 11.59 pm call, which lasted 45 seconds, on 20 June 2009. It is reasonable to assume that this unidentified caller was fully aware that Krystal was no longer in a position to receive calls. Despite the detective's appeal for the caller to identify themselves that person has never taken up the invitation.

Sometime after this Karen Fraser said she received a phone call from a detective who identified himself as Rod Stewart from Bendigo CIU. She said she remembers the name because she jokingly asked him to sing her a song. Karen said that Stewart apologised to her, saying that he didn't know of her existence because Brady had led them to believe that Krystal only had an elderly grandmother.

Despite this officer's apparent unawareness of Krystal's immediate family members, the question remains, why wasn't there any police follow up with Krystal's grandmother, who made the missing person's report? Karen said Detective Stewart also indicated that the local member (Brady) had encouraged them to accept that Krystal was hiding out somewhere interstate.

During my research I had a conversation with Crossley, currently a detective senior sergeant in regional Victoria. During this discussion he disputed the timing of the CIU's involvement in the case, which I had based on the August media reference to his office. He argued that his office was involved in the investigation from the beginning, as doing a risk rating (assessment) on all missing persons is part of the CIU's role in the investigation of crime. He said the risk rating made on Krystal was 'high risk' based on her intellectual disability. There was no reference to her advanced pregnancy or the likelihood of a baby. He said that he conducted background checks on all her associates, had CCRs (call charge records) from her phone, so knew all of these, stressing that everyone who had a relationship with Krystal was interviewed and/or checked out.

Despite his resolve at that time that his office was involved in Krystal's disappearance from the outset; evidence he gave at Krystal's inquest (13 July 2022) contradicts this. His evidence there was that he first became involved in the investigation on 22 July 2009 because 'all missing persons cases, once they went past thirty days, the CIU would usually be notified to have a look at it.' He said he was briefed by Brady on that day and attended at Krystal's flat '…to get a feel for what was happening and whether there was anything unusual or suspicious in the unit. There was, the whole time, at the commencement of our involvement, a significant emphasis that Krystal had run away.…'

During his evidence Crossley said that he remembered hearing rumours that Krystal's child was going to be taken from her by DHS. He never suggested that Brady told him this, nor did he disclose if he made any enquiries with DHS himself. Had he done so, he may have dismissed this as a reason for Krystal's disappearance.

Crossley noted at the time of his search that there were '... no signs of disturbance, the main bed was folded back like someone had just got out of it and all of Krystal's clothing was in drawers in the master bedroom, dishes were washed and in a drying rack on the sink.'

Unknown to him, and to other investigators to follow, was the fact that the bedding and clothes had been cleaned after Krystal's disappearance but before their visits.

He also stated that in a plastic bag on a lounge chair he found Krystal's wallet along with a bottle of chocolate topping and two miniature board games, two $5 notes and a train ticket from Bendigo to Pyramid Hill dated 20 June 2009. He advised that no forensic analysis was undertaken on that occasion. Crossley said he seized the wallet, Krystal's computer and two address books.

Brady, although not maintaining a log of his activities, briefed Crossley that he had spoken to Robert Glennie, the man Krystal visited after getting off the train; and had searched his and Jason McPherson's premises. McPherson was identified by Brady as being a regular visitor to Krystal and in phone contact with her on the night of her disappearance. Brady also told him about Krystal's apparent relationship with Tony Gatt from Bendigo. Crossley said he went to Gatt's home and when he wasn't there spoke to him later on the phone.

Brady also told him that he had arranged for Bendigo uniform police to visit a Gareth David, another person identified as an acquaintance of Krystal, who was also not able to help with the inquiry. Brady had also spoken to Nicholas Dingfelder who had contacted him and advised him that he had observed Krystal leaving the train. Crossley also gave evidence that Brady told him he had notified the person responsible for Krystal from DHS.

Crossley said that he also submitted requests for Krystal's CCRs for her phone and believes he received them in the first week of his involvement in the investigation (which suggests that Brady could have obtained them just as promptly from the outset). Crossley gave evidence that as soon as he learned that Krystal's phone had stopped early in the morning of 21 June 2009 and '...there was no activity on her phone, it started arousing suspicions that something may have happened to her.'

The Fraser family had been pressing this point for more than a month at this stage, emphasising Krystal's prolific use of her phone before 20 June 2009 and the complete lack of contact since. Crossley said they were unaware of the Leitchville phone box calls for another week, until they obtained reverse CCRs with details of calls made to Krystal.

Commenting on the Leitchville phone box calls, Crossley said they observed that Peter Jenkinson had been constantly on the phone with Krystal and these calls had stopped the day before the calls from the post office had begun and '...this aroused suspicion with us.' A media release asking for the caller to come forward was circulated as a result.

Crossley gave evidence that Brady had previously tasked

the Gunbower police officer to speak to Peter Jenkinson upon learning that he had been a friend of Krystal. Crossley said that Detective Lloyd Twycross from his office had also contacted Jenkinson, via telephone only, during their investigation and Jenkinson stated that he had known Krystal for a number of years and hadn't spoken to her for six weeks and had last seen her two to three months ago.

A former detective, who I have chosen not to name and who was at Bendigo CIU during the preliminary stages of the investigation into Krystal's disappearance, contributed to the dialogue about the investigation with, 'The copper from there who was rooting her was a suspect for a while.' Asked if he was referring to Brady, he replied, 'The lack of initial action by Brady made it a mess for investigators for an awfully long time. Unfortunately, he just didn't know what he was doing and this impacted on what was being done and on what he was reporting to us. He failed to do stuff and if he did do stuff or learn anything, he failed to document or share it. It was amazing he didn't get into the shit; he was on the fringe of getting in the shit the whole time he was there.'

While it should be acknowledged that this officer was not involved in the case it does suggest that the case and Brady's performance were evaluated within the Bendigo CIU office.

Despite Bendigo CIU's proprietorship of the investigation by then a further post on 10 August in the *Bendigo Advertiser* reported, 'VP hold grave fears for the safety of missing Bendigo woman Krystal Fraser and her baby, who may have travelled to New South Wales.' The statement provided the public with the continued vague notion that Krystal was possibly 'just a runaway'; a characterisation likely to have stymied public support. The article also continued to erroneously refer to Krystal as being missing from Bendigo, which again was likely to have impacted on the public's attention and awareness.

The police airwing conducted a general search of the Pyramid Hill area at this time, the search yielding nothing. Another search, involving mainly volunteers was conducted before this on the iconic 'hill' overlooking the Pyramid Hill golf course. The objective of the search, according to a police officer involved, was to locate Krystal's body. It would be most extraordinary for a killer seeking to dispose of a body to carry it up such a very steep gradient as this site. Particularly one that is an extremely popular tourist destination. An ascent of the hill revealed litter in virtually every crevice, indicating the area's extensive use that makes it a highly undesirable site for disposal of a body.

While acknowledging occasional phone contact with detectives from Bendigo, Krystal's immediate family said none of them were ever spoken to on a face-to-face basis by members of this office during their investigation.

Brady conceded recently that it was his belief that Krystal was hiding out until he was made aware by members of Bendigo CIU of the details of the phone calls being made to Krystal from the Leitchville phone box. He admitted that before this, 'My first thoughts were that the family had hidden the kid because Karen wanted that baby so badly.'

Brady's fallacious and unshakeable attitude to the circumstances surrounding Krystal's disappearance would have clearly influenced both his own and the hypotheses of other police overseeing the case. The failure of Bendigo detectives to interview Helen Fraser, the reporting family member, and Krystal's immediate family, validates this view. Where were police involved in this case getting their intel? Phone records can only offer so much. The family were clearly in the best position to provide information about Krystal and her history to assist police in their investigation.

Police officers involved in a case of this nature also have another responsibility, namely, to provide support for the family in their time of fear and anxiety. The Frasers suggest the first words of support they heard were from homicide squad officers after the family had apparently been eliminated as suspects.

While the police involved may not have had any news for the family, the importance of contact and reassurance that things were being done and avenues of enquiry being explored clearly would have reduced the sense of isolation and loneliness the family have endured. There can be no excuse for the lack of empathy and concern shown for the Fraser family during the early stages of the investigation into Krystal's disappearance.

CHAPTER SEVEN

A Homicide Squad Investigation

There was no further media coverage of Krystal's disappearance for more than two months; it is possible that investigators were interviewing those identified through Krystal's phone records and following any subsequent leads originating from same during this period.

Media coverage of the matter resumed on 15 October 2009 with, 'Police believe a Bendigo woman who went missing days before she was due to give birth has been murdered. Homicide squad detectives have taken over the investigation into the disappearance of missing Bendigo woman Krystal Fraser. Investigators now believe she has been murdered.' (*Bendigo Advertiser*).

Det-Sgt Wayne Woltsche of the homicide squad was identified as the officer in charge of the investigation. He was cited saying that the (unidentified) person who made the midnight call to Krystal's mobile on the day of her disappearance was the focus of their inquiries. He was further quoted, '...the homicide squad has become involved in Ms Fraser's disappearance although no new evidence has been uncovered.' Is this acquiescence that they should have been onboard back in June following Krystal's mysterious disappearance?

Although the public were only made aware of the homicide squad's involvement in the case midway through October 2009, Wayne Woltsche provided evidence at the inquest into Krystal's disappearance that he was briefed by Detective Crossley on 7 August. During his evidence he said that following the earlier disbanding of the missing persons squad, missing persons who were considered possible homicides had become the responsibility of the homicide squad. He stated that he viewed it as a homicide from the outset based on the circumstances, and the telephone records in particular.

Woltsche said he spoke to Brady on 13 August and realised his investigation was based on Krystal turning up alive and his endeavours had only been to find her. It was a view that Woltsche believed was shared by other police until the Bendigo CIU quickly came to the conclusion that something had happened to Krystal. Woltsche said they did a door knock in Kelly Street, Pyramid Hill, and considered those identified in the initial stages; Robert Glennie, Allan Summers (Bandy) and Craig Newton, another person known to have been in the company of Krystal just before her disappearance.

Woltsche said he never believed Krystal was at risk of running away to avoid DHS, '...she was, from all reports, comfortable in the final week at the Medihotel and there was no indication to staff, family or friends that she would run away.'

The coroner, Katherine Lorenz, asked Woltsche what would have been done differently if Krystal's disappearance had been treated as foul play from the outset. He said, 'Things would have been done different, we would have been able to lock people into a story, with accurate times, dates, and places. It would have prevented rumour and innuendo, the biggest difficulty we had was getting people to remember what they did six weeks earlier.'

It is obvious that people will forget facts over time. Stories change, people's stories also adapt based on what they've heard from others. Fixing a person, particularly a suspect, to a story with times, dates, places, and people is extremely important.

* * *

A *Bendigo Advertiser* article on 16 October 2009 refers to homicide squad detectives and forty volunteers searching a property ten kilometres east of Pyramid Hill the previous day after receiving a tip-off about the location of Krystal's body.

I have established that this property was located in McRae Road, just off the Pyramid Hill-Leitchville Road, northeast of Pyramid Hill. Karen Fraser said Detective Senior Constable Sharon Bell, a member of the homicide crew conducting the inquiry, had rung her and advised her that the search was going to take place. Nothing was found during this search which is understood to have been conducted based on two separate tipoffs that Krystal's body had been dumped there. More on this property later.

Additional relevant details were released the following day in the *Herald Sun* of 17 October 2009, with Det-Sgt Woltsche saying, 'About 1.30 to 1.45 am she was online, or someone she was with was using her phone to access the internet. But again, without the phone, we don't have any information on what sites were accessed.'

The *Sunday Herald Sun*, on 25 October 2009 offers the first piece of noteworthy evidence with the following: 'Two days before nine-months pregnant Krystal Fraser disappeared, she told a friend online she feared the father of her child would harm her if she gave birth.' The article identified Carlo Anfuso, a building contractor of Bendigo, as the source of this latest information.

I found Carlo and learned that he was aged about eighteen or nineteen when he first interacted with Krystal. He said this was through a website chat line operated by Telstra and known as AirG, which provided users with the ability to communicate in private via their mobile phone for free. It offered voice communication only. Carlo accepted that he joined the chat line to 'meet girls, pre Tinder.' He said Krystal was friendly and outgoing during their online conversations and after a short time he arranged to travel to Pyramid Hill to meet and get to know her. He said that on arrival at the prearranged coffee shop he was shocked to see that Krystal was heavily pregnant. He acknowledged he had had no desire to know a pregnant woman, saying, 'I was looking for fun, not a permanent relationship.' He also conceded, 'I was also put off by, a little scared even, by her intellectual disability that was apparent when I met her.'(A recurring theme in Krystal's life). He said they had a coffee and he returned home to Bendigo.

He said he continued to communicate with Krystal via the chat line but tried to give her the impression that he wasn't interested without hurting her feelings, telling her that he wanted to remain friends but nothing more. He claimed Krystal became quite obsessive and pushy but despite this she continued to communicate with him online. Carlo recalled that the last occasion on which he spoke to Krystal was during the week of her disappearance.

While the *Sunday Herald Sun* article referred to this conversation as being two days before her disappearance, he said he is not sure if it was two days or more but is confident it was less than a week beforehand. He said in all their communication previously, Krystal had never spoken about the father of her baby and similarly had never mentioned a boyfriend or boyfriends. However, during this final conversation, just before the pending birth of her baby, he said she told him that the father of the baby had told her that he would get rid of her if she had the baby. He said he queried what she meant by this and that Krystal had replied, 'kill me.'

He said he was shocked by this, adding that Krystal had seemed stressed throughout this chat. Asked how the media became aware of this information he said he assumed the homicide squad provided his details to the newspaper (highly unlikely). He further advised he had given a statement to police a couple of months before this after he saw an article mentioning Krystal's continued absence.

There is only one other reporting of this murder investigation during 2009. A brief synopsis appeared in the *Bendigo Advertiser* on 19 December containing no fresh information. Notice of an application for a $100,000 reward appeared in the *Herald Sun* on 10 June 2010, and the only added information referenced is that Krystal's phone was being used to 'surf the internet from 1.30 am to 3.00 am.' Previously it had been reported that it had been used for this purpose between 1.30 am and 1.35 am (on Sunday 21 June 2009).

An *Age* article of 23 June 2012, prepared by Chris Johnston and Nino Bucci, provided the most comprehensive commentary on the case to date. Published on the third anniversary of Krystal's disappearance, the piece suggested that homicide detectives believed she was murdered because she was over-friendly. Either a nebulous interpretation by the journalists or an elusive insight offered by detectives. It also records that, 'Locals reckon there is a prime suspect. His name is rarely mentioned now, but it is whispered.'

The journalists appear to have been told this person's identity because the report followed up with, 'I've got nothing to say about it. I gave them (the homicide squad) all the information I could, and they've used it against me. It's turned my life upside down. They've tried to turn my mates against me.'

Pyramid Hill locals have speculated and homicide detectives have confirmed to the Fraser family that this person was Peter Jenkinson. Det-Sgt Woltsche is quoted in the article, 'Whose baby is it and how do you prove that, unless we find her? No-one has ever admitted they are the father of the child to us, but a number of people have admitted they have had relationships with her. Those involved with Krystal did so largely in secret; friends now realise she had a double life.'

The article continued with the suggestion that two other suspects identified were, '...red herrings, a distracting clue which turns out to be wrong.' Both committed suicide within several months of Krystal's disappearance. One, a man who lived in the same housing commission block of units as Krystal and was alleged to have been arguing with her before she disappeared, killed himself by lying in front of a train on the nearby railway tracks.

Karen Fraser responded to the suggestion of an argument with the following, '...they had had an altercation; I think it was basically a clash of personalities. He was a weirdo, mental health issues, but it had nothing to do with Krystal. He was interviewed but should never have been considered a suspect, and the dispute took place well before Krystal's disappearance.'

The other 'suspect' referred to was Stephen Jones, who shot himself by the Pyramid Creek near Kerang on 27 May 2010. He was a truck driver for the McGillivray abattoir in Gunbower at the time. One of the many rumours abounding suggested Krystal's body had been disposed of at the abattoir, minced and fed to pigs. Jones was considered a suspect for a time and eliminated. There is no indication as to why he was considered a suspect other than the possibility that telephone records may have shown regular contact between Krystal and him before her disappearance. Based on the broad exposure of Detective Woltsche's personal history throughout the article, the comment that these suspects were nothing more than red herrings, seems to have been contributed by him.

During a meeting between Woltsche and Karen Fraser where she was briefed about the homicide squad's activities she said that Woltsche told her that his team weren't pursuing any drug enquiries and had been telling people that they were not interested in the drugs, only the person or persons responsible for Krystal's disappearance.

Karen was surprised by this and told Woltsche as much, suggesting that if evidence of drug dealing was uncovered against suspects in the case that this could be used as leverage to obtain information relating to Krystal. This seems a reasonable proposition and is a method often used by investigators to obtain a result in the more significant aspect of a case by applying legitimate pressure where a weakness has been exposed.

CHAPTER EIGHT

Pyramid Hill

Pyramid Hill, or Pyramid, as the locals refer to it, is a small agricultural services town in the Loddon shire named by explorer Major Thomas Mitchell in 1836. Viewing the impressive granite formation on the edge of town it is obvious how the locality got its name. Rising out of a flat landscape to a height of about 180 metres, the hill takes the form of a pyramid, especially from a distance. It is nowhere near as imposing as Uluru but impressive, nonetheless.

The town supports a now stable population of a little more than four hundred. An ongoing steady decline in residents has been averted over the last ten years by an influx of Filipino migrants who now make up twenty-five per cent of the population. A large piggery, cropping, sheep production and the mining of gold, salt and granite are the main economic drivers.

Indicative of a small rural town supported by farming are ads carried in the community tabloid, the *Pyramid Hill Press*, which includes offerings of farm machinery and repairs, seed cleaning, water trading and deliveries, rural fencing, chook sales, rural financial counselling, mobile sheep dipping, fox baiting, firewood and Landcare, along with those from the local pub, bakery and, predictably, funeral services.

As in many small towns, the local footy club is a focal point of the community, providing social connection and support, personal development and civic pride. Sometimes seen as a business rival, the club, known as the Bulldogs, is a large consumer within the local community. In times of economic hardship, however, local loyalties can be tested. For example, the club advertises a load of firewood for $140 while a small business enterprise offers the same for $110, having the potential of creating disputes.

While there are a few handsome buildings in the township, including the Memorial Hall, the Victoria Hotel and the art deco supermarket, there are many dilapidated and empty former business premises.

Locals pretty well sustain the small business enterprises, but this might have more to do with the town's isolation from a major retail centre than communal allegiances. All Pyramid Hill's neighbouring settlements are small. Anyone in need of a major supermarket chain, a national fast-food outlet, live music, cinema or fine dining faces a round trip of 150 kilometres via minor C class rural roads to the regional city of Echuca.

In spring, the area is covered in wildflowers and the views across the pastures from the top of the 'hill,' as the locals refer to it, are engaging. There is a picturesque eighteen-hole golf club encircling its base and picnic tables and public toilets are situated alongside the trail to the summit. The 'hill' provides hiking opportunities as do nearby Mt Hope and Terrick National Park. These natural landscapes provide plenty of wildlife, including a hundred species of native birds.

According to a number of long-term residents the town's character has been considerably transformed over the last fifteen years. While the vast majority are enthusiastic about the arrival of the Filipino migrants, they are less so about a new breed of 'losers' who have been arriving steadily throughout that time. Ostensibly, this sub-group do not work or participate in or embrace a sense of community, and disregards common social mores. They also are said to be drug and alcohol abusers. The former local co-publican, David Demaine, who operated the pub for more than twelve years with his wife, including at the time of Krystal's disappearance, referred to this group as 'ratbags.' Another businessperson labelled them 'rats, dopeheads and useless lazy pricks.'

An earlier murder of local resident Anne Watson, who was stabbed, strangled and set alight by her husband, James, in their Pyramid Hill home, was front of mind in the town with news of James's conviction on 24 June 2009 — the same day that news of Krystal's status as missing became public. Within a short period of time a universal fear spread through the town that Krystal may have suffered a similar fate. Locals described the feeling in the town at the time as sombre and, as each day passed without any news of Krystal, the mood darkened. Long term Pyramid Hill residents now generally do not want to discuss the case, the town equally divided between one of two beliefs. Namely, that either the police had the right person in the gun without laying charges or the killer committed suicide many years ago. Of those in the former camp the identity of the offender is not a universal one. Those believing the offender took their own life point to Stephen Jones but, as concluded by the homicide investigators, the evidence doesn't. A number of people believe there are people in the town who have vital information that they have shared openly with others, but which they have refused to disclose to police, or to the Fraser family. Others are accused of simply lying to police to protect their friends or through fear of reprisal.

There are also those that speak of a police cover-up, orchestrated by Brady to prevent the exposure of an assumed relationship with Krystal. Some people also wrongly consider him a suspect in Krystal's disappearance, alleging he may have been the father of her unborn child. The argument here is that he was able to control the investigation and direct attention away from the fact that Krystal was the victim of a serious crime by continuously suggesting she was simply hiding out.

Wayne Woltsche of the homicide squad told the Fraser family that Brady was considered a suspect briefly, but then eliminated. The exculpatory evidence available to exclude Brady is unknown, but he told me that he was watching the

AFL game on television with friends at their house on the night of Krystal's disappearance. He also provided me with the name of the householder.

The suggestions that Brady's reputation had deteriorated before Krystal's disappearance as a consequence of allegations of heavy drinking, various intimate partners, big noting and lack of professionalism are alleged to have caused some locals to avoid him, simply not trusting him or at best unwilling to communicate with him. It is also a real possibility though that only one person is aware of what happened to Krystal and that person has kept their mouth shut.

* * *

I spent more than twenty-seven years with Victoria Police and most of my policing career was devoted to investigative work. This included service in the CIB, including with a specialist crime squad and metro and regional criminal investigation divisions. This was followed by seven years in charge of a district support group and then as a detective inspector at the corruption investigation division of the ethical standards department.

Early in my career I was stationed at Rochester and, as a result, am familiar with Pyramid Hill. Our policing boundaries extended towards one another across thousands of hectares of lightly inhabited wheat-belts. I reference this to illustrate why I maintained an interest in Krystal's case.

I had lived and policed in a small rural area not dissimilar to Pyramid Hill and felt that when in this position I had a particularly good grasp of anything a little dodgy, or not quite right happening on my patch.

Following my retirement from VicPol, I operated businesses in Swan Hill and occasionally took the train to Melbourne that stopped at the tiny hamlet of Pyramid Hill. I remember trying to see if any passengers ever got on or off the train, for it seemed to only stop for mere seconds before it was on its way again. I believe, it was this sense of transient connection with the town that continued to pique my interest in Krystal's case.

I first read about the disappearance of Krystal Fraser from Pyramid Hill in 2009 while living in Swan Hill. Like many old coppers I wondered if the investigation was making any progress. Concern for victims is an inherent quality in most effective investigators, serving or retired. I remember thinking at the time, based on the details released to the public, that there shouldn't have been a large pool of suspects given the size of Krystal's hometown and its apparent isolation from a major regional centre. Krystal's lack of mobility contributed to my belief that the matter would be quickly resolved.

I continued to read the odd detail about the case over the following few years, wondering why the circumstances behind Krystal's disappearance hadn't been resolved. As the investigation had become a homicide squad enquiry there must surely have been evidence indicating she had been murdered.

After selling our businesses in Swan Hill I retired to Echuca, the move coinciding with the tenth anniversary of Krystal's disappearance. I recall that for the first time in years there was significant media coverage of the case, such as I'd never seen previously. I read everything I could find on the mystery at the time, which also gained great exposure in Echuca's local paper, the *Riverine Herald*. The media spotlight included a media conference at the Bendigo police station on 17 July 2019, and the announcement of a $1 million reward leading to the conviction of those responsible for Krystal's disappearance.

I felt that this shift in the investigation meant one of two things; police had a good suspect and needed a little more that they hoped the reward offer might spawn, or they had bugger all and this was a last gasp attempt to resuscitate the investigation. The tone of the police media release suggested the former. It was reported that new information had led to a person of interest identified earlier in the investigation again becoming the focus of the investigation. Over the following few months, I studied media reporting of the case online. Despite the reward and fresh media attention, it appeared pretty obvious that there had been no resolution in the case.

I was concerned that there didn't seem to be an active investigation under way, and no answers to the circumstances of Krystal's disappearance, her whereabouts, and who was responsible. I thought that given the enormous amount of free time I then had plus my previous investigative experience — including murders — that I might be able to make my own enquiries in the hope that I might be able to provide some comfort to the Fraser family.

I accepted that I had no official authority to conduct an investigation but was also aware that we are all free to ask questions of anyone else. I appreciated that I needed a mechanism to justify knocking on people's doors, to afford me some form of legitimacy. I decided that I could accomplish this by writing a book about the case, believing this would give me the authenticity required. My solitary motivation for this was hopefully to provide solace for the Fraser family.

CHAPTER NINE

The Frasers

Before the Frasers were made aware that the homicide squad had taken over Krystal's investigation, Karen received a call from a good friend in Pyramid Hill who said, 'There are blokes in suits, cops I'd say, and they're going through your garden beds with sticks.' The family was still operating their confectionary business from Horsham at this time. Following the 'clandestine' search of their property, Wayne Woltsche, the senior investigating officer rang Karen and invited her and Neil in for a discussion about the case at the Pyramid Hill police station. The timing of this is believed to have been mid-September 2009.

Karen said when they arrived at their local cop shop to speak to the investigators she was surprised when they were split up and taken into separate interview rooms. Karen said she was spoken to by Det-Sen-Constable Sharon Bell. Karen said that she seemed nice, compassionate and friendly. 'She asked me questions about Krystal and my thoughts about what had happened to her. This went on for about half an hour, all very courteous and polite. I couldn't provide her with anything more than sharing some of the rumours that were circulating about the possibility of the father of Krystal's baby being responsible, but I was unable to tell her who this was. All of a sudden, she turned into a bully, slamming her fist down on the desk in front of me and yelling, 'What have you done with Krystal. No more of your bullshit.'

Karen said she initially burst into tears with the shock at the words used by the officer but quickly composed herself and said, 'You're the one full of bullshit, love.'

Neil said he was interviewed by Woltsche and experienced a similar encounter. He was told he was the chief suspect in Krystal's disappearance on the basis of statistics indicating that family and friends were responsible in the vast majority of such cases. Neil told him to do his homework and check the Wimmera Base Hospital in-patient records before making false accusations. Woltsche told him that he had.

Karen revealed, 'Unfortunately, this stuff got around town and the locals gossiped about us being involved, it was bloody awful, we had enough to deal with without this happening. It was insensitive and obviously wrong.'

It is not known what, if any, evidence the homicide investigators had to engage in this pantomime but as the hypothesis never arose again Karen Fraser figured that it was simply a matter of addressing the possibility and putting it to bed.

* * *

Chapter Nine   The Frasers

It was abundantly clear that Karen Fraser, Krystal's mother had been the family's only contact with the media. Her father, Neil, had never been quoted in any media channels as far as I could discern. I accepted that to conduct a thorough examination of Krystal's disappearance I had to speak to Karen.

I knew she still lived in Pyramid Hill but not her address. I initially made contact with Joy Jenkins, the then senior constable in charge of Pyramid Hill police station. I introduced myself to Joy and advised her of my desire to draft a book about Krystal's disappearance. I asked her if she would mind passing on my details to Karen Fraser and to advise her that I hoped my enquiries would generate fresh discussion about the case which might lead to evidence against the person or persons responsible.

Joy's initial feedback was that Karen appeared interested. But this was clearly not the case as Karen failed to call me. I didn't want to burn any bridges with Joy Jenkins or put her at risk of censure from her superiors by asking her to do anything else for me. I also never asked her what she knew about the case for the same reason.

I then made contact with the missing persons squad, which had been reinstated and in 2018 had assumed responsibility for Krystal's case from the homicide squad. I spoke to Det.-Acting-Sen-Sgt Maurice Ryan. I informed him of my plans and sought an introduction from his office to Karen Fraser for the purpose of obtaining material for the book.

I never asked for any details of the case, simply the

possibility of an introduction. He declined. I then forwarded an email to him requesting some generic information about his squad, namely, number of active cases being worked, official designation of Krystal's investigation and the number of detectives in this division. Within two hours I received an email reply from Andrew Stamper, the detective inspector in charge of the missing persons squad. He asked me to refrain from directing questions to his members, advising me to make any requests to the media and corporate communications department of Victoria Police. I took his advice and was told by a member of this department that an official FOI request would be required and the process could be a long one. This person, in sympathy I guess, said that the reality was that my request would end up with the officer in charge of the missing persons squad who would decline it anyway. A dog chasing its tail.

I was running out of options but not ideas. I canvassed the occupants of houses in Findlay Avenue, Leitchville, the location of the phone box where the calls, including the final one, were made to Krystal's mobile. I also conducted my own door to door enquiries within the vicinity of Krystal's old flat in Kelly Street, Pyramid Hill. I attempted to find the previous owner of the Pyramid Hill pub, who had been quoted in articles covering the case over the years. I learned later that the publicans were great mates with the Frasers. Details of my enquiries were getting back to Karen Fraser and unfortunately it seems she was far from happy about it.

My good mate Bob Kerr knew of my intentions to draft the book and offered to help where he could. Given the frustrations I was experiencing in getting access to the Frasers, I sought his help. Bob and I were detectives together in Mildura in the 1980s and again at the corruption investigation division at the end of our policing careers. Bob is married to Kim, also a retired officer with an extensive criminal investigation background. As I wasn't a Facebook user I tasked Bob, who is, to examine the 'Help us find Krystal Fraser' Facebook group for possible leads.

Bob established that the Facebook group was administered by Chantel Fraser, Krystal's younger sister. I asked Bob to make contact with Chantel in an effort to gain access to her mother, Karen, so that I could speak to her personally. Chantel was told that my hope was to stimulate interest in the case through a book and thus help solve the mystery of Krystal's disappearance.

Chantel advised that she was living in Queensland and obviously not in a position to meet. After a further appeal to her via Facebook, she responded on behalf of the entire family stating that they did not want a book to be written about Krystal and that the Pyramid Hill community did not wish to comment either. She added that the investigation was still active and it might be compromised by a book. She asked that I stop speaking to people in Pyramid Hill.

I then wrote a letter to Karen Fraser apologising for my efforts in trying to speak to her. I also advised her that I intended to continue making enquiries in an attempt to bring about a resolution in the case. I referred to the comments made by Chantel in her latest communication about my enquiries jeopardising the investigation telling her that any new leads or evidence would be directed immediately to investigators.

Having by this stage established the Frasers' address I hand delivered the letter, not expecting, but hoping, to meet Karen or Neil. Karen met me at the front door and instantly recognised my name. She said as it was still an active investigation she did not wish to discuss it. She added, 'I'm between a rock and a hard place here, you've gotta realise I've had eleven years of all this stuff. Look I loved my daughter and miss her dreadfully. I've dealt with the media and they just twist things and say all these horrible things and I'm just not willing to do it. I want the police to solve it. I think it should have been solved. So I just have to sit tight. It's frustrating but I'm just a simple mum. I don't know the pros and cons of what you are or aren't allowed to do. Sen-Constable Brady, the local bloke initially responsible for the matter, is no longer in the police force, surprise, surprise. He threw me out of the case, I'm her mum. Comments about Krystal being interstate and hiding out with her baby were coming out of his arse, I don't know. He had this big thing that because Krystal had issues, and this is the bit that really pisses me off, their putting it out there, not the police but the media, that she was retarded and so I've copped a lot of flak from that. Why did I let her get pregnant? I had no control. I organised an implant in her arm so that she couldn't get pregnant but it obviously failed. Then they portrayed her as a nutter and that she smelt and was a serial pest. Jason Brady fucked it up plain and simple.'

Karen accepted my letter in which I offered a further apology for upsetting her by trying to make contact with her through others. I stressed that my interests were the same as hers in seeking answers to the tragedy. I encouraged her to help me fill in the blanks, potentially opening up new avenues of enquiry and subsequently limiting my enquiries outside the family.

I raised my concerns that the stigma applied to people with a disability, which marginalises them and contributes to a vulnerability to abuse, may have impacted on the investigation and the willingness of people to come forward. I also emphasised the disparity in the level of media exposure Krystal received compared to other victims.

Two days after my meeting with Karen, Bob received a Facebook message from Chantel revealing that she had spoken to her mum again and that as the anniversary of Krystal's disappearance was fast approaching they would get a lot of people contacting them for stories and she just wanted to protect her mother.

There was a distinct shift in Chantel's tone, however, writing that if I was serious about what I'd written in my letter to Karen she would need to see some proof of Bob and my policing backgrounds. She also asked for a list of questions, indicating that she would discuss them with Karen and then decide if they would proceed with an interview.

Despite that tempered response, two weeks later Chantel messaged Bob saying that the family were declining our request. 'We do not wish to proceed with having a book written that has no ending.' Bob responded on my behalf with advice that I would continue to seek information from other sources, despite their rejection.

Within a couple of days, however, Chantel informed us that she was prepared to participate in the book. No reason was given at the time, but she told me later that she had discussed my intentions with her partner, Adam, a former resident of Swan Hill. After he told her he knew my son and I and that we were okay, she changed her mind. I didn't personally know Adam but established that we had work done on our company vehicles where he had worked in Swan Hill.

In order to facilitate more efficient communication with Chantel and Bob we created a WhatsApp group account. Following this, Chantel and I established a close working relationship, albeit that it was all via technology as Chantel resided interstate.

Covid travel restrictions and lockdowns delayed my opportunities to visit those identified as potential sources of information. Where possible, I visited individuals without prior warning, appreciating that if people were prewarned they may reject a meeting. I only rang first if I didn't know the person's address. I visited a few who don't appear in the book, some refused to speak to me, others had nothing to contribute, and one provided a credible story in relation to Krystal's disappearance and the location of her body.

I forwarded this witness's account to the missing persons squad, as I told the witness I would, but the squad never contacted the person. The Frasers didn't think the information was plausible but when the MPS failed to contact the witness I felt they must have established the identity of Krystal's killer; why else would they not have jumped all over this latest information?

After finally gaining the family's trust I was granted my first interview with Karen Fraser. Chantel warned me before the meeting that Karen would have a friend with her during this process. I was surprised when I arrived at Karen's house to find two extra women there. Karen introduced the women as follows, 'These are my two best friends, Debbie Demaine, my voice of reason, and Tanya Quinn, my bullshit detector. Without the love and support of these two women I would not have coped with Krystal's loss, I would have simply gone mad.'

I spent several hours talking to Karen and her friends. Despite the passage of time, Karen was still deeply distraught about the loss of Krystal. Her distress was shared by her good friends who clearly had her back. There were a lot of tears and I couldn't help being affected by the collective sadness, but there was also laughter amid tales of Krystal's capers.

When I asked Karen to describe the types of men Krystal had had relationships with, she said, 'The worst kind of men and there were plenty of them. Look Krystal was my daughter and while she could be pretty, she hid her femininity, wearing her hair really short and dressing like a boy. She also had crooked teeth and a deep voice so I don't know why so many men slept with her. But Krystal used sex to have friends, knowing that if she were nice to some bloke and wanted him to be nice to her, she would have to sleep with him. And she did.'

During the early stages of the investigation into Krystal's disappearance the Frasers continued to spend the majority of their working week operating their confectionary business out of Horsham, returning home to Pyramid Hill on weekends. Karen said that while they received regular updates from Wayne Woltsche, the investigation didn't seem to be making any progress. She said that Neil and she tried to carry on with their lives, as recommended by close friends and by Woltsche.

She recalled one Friday night at the local pub Karen said a local told her that she should've been out looking for her daughter instead of partying in the pub. Karen said she told the woman, 'That's why we have a police force, I wouldn't know where to start looking, they're the ones that need to get their fingers out of their arses and do their job. We might have learnt something by now if Jason Brady hadn't have fucked it up from the start.'

Karen said she felt many locals didn't understand or appreciate the impact Krystal's disappearance was having on their lives and continued to have on their lives. She said that a number of people who had been friends previously didn't know how to respond to her as the mother of a missing daughter and she came to realise that she was a changed person as a result. She said many people didn't even want to mention Krystal for fear of upsetting her and others wanted to know everything, perhaps in the interests of sharing with others; she wasn't quite sure after a while.

Karen said that relationships have changed over time and that she now has three close friends with whom she does everything and admits that she no longer feels part of the community she has lived in for more than thirty years. She acknowledged that without these three close friends her life would be very lonely.

When I asked if she had ever sought any counselling for her grief, she said, 'Wayne Woltsche told me there was counselling available. I spoke to a counsellor; Priscilla was her name. She rang me and asked me what she could do to help and I told her that she could tell me where my daughter was. She said that she didn't have those answers and I told her that if that was the case she was of no use to me. I just need to speak to someone who can tell me where my daughter is.'

* * *

The Frasers told me that one of the first people taken into custody as a suspect in Krystal's disappearance was Craig

Newton, who was also known as 'Twiggy' Newton. Newton had been identified as having been a close acquaintance of and potentially in a relationship with Krystal in the months before her disappearance. They were regularly in contact via mobile phone and he was a visitor to her flat in Pyramid Hill.

Newton, who was on long-term unemployment benefits and living with his partner of several years, Susan and their three children, was living in Cohuna at the time. A previous partner, identified as Cathy, not her real name, was living on a farm property on Gladfield South Road, about six kilometres south of Pyramid Hill. She was then married to Wayne (also not his real name), with whom she lived with their six children, three of whom were fathered by Craig Newton.

Karen Fraser said Detective Sharon Bell told her that Newton had confessed during an interview with homicide officers. Karen said she asked Bell to provide more details, eager to locate Krystal. She said that Bell said, 'Oh, he would only take the story so far and then clam up. There wasn't enough to charge him at the time and we are making further enquiries.'

Karen said she couldn't fathom this. 'How could someone make a confession and not be charged?'

The family lived with this paradox for almost ten years until Det-Sen-Constable Damon Abby of the missing persons squad, who at the time identified himself to Karen and Neil as being in charge of the case, advised them that Newton had simply made some belligerent comment during an interview and that it was not a confession at all.

That knowledge might have been useful to the Fraser family years earlier and prevented a confrontation at the Pyramid Hill Hotel. A short time after the family were told about this 'confession' Karen and her daughter Chantel went to the pub and saw Newton there with his daughter, Jasmine, whom Chantel also knew. Chantel said that she and Karen were drinking in the beer garden at the rear of the pub and Newton and his daughter were seated at the bar inside.

Chantel said whenever she or her mum walked past the Newtons, Jasmine made 'snarky' remarks about them blaming Newton for Krystal's death. Karen said she was able to maintain her composure and ignore them. However, Chantel admits that she cracked and hissed at Jasmine, 'Stop sitting there high and mighty, if he doesn't want people pointing the finger at him he shouldn't have made a confession.' Chantel said, 'Jasmine said something like, "Fuck off you stupid bitch" and we faced off for a time before I returned to mum outside and told her what was said.' Chantel said her mother suggested that it was time to go and they left the pub.

Chantel said she was also troubled at the time by the fact that Newton had 'accepted' a Facebook friend request from Krystal on 5 August 2009. It has not been established when Krystal generated the request, but it was unequivocally evident to everyone who knew Krystal that she was no longer around by the time of his acceptance.

Chantel had suspected Newton of being responsible for Krystal's disappearance from the beginning. She said Krystal had told her that she was running drugs for Newton, and others, couriering them between Pyramid Hill and Bendigo on the train. Suspicions of Newton's role as a drug dealer were widely acknowledged in Pyramid Hill according to Chantel and she couldn't understand why Brady and Newton talked to one another in the pub and 'seemed matey.'

She felt Brady had to have known Newton was a suspected drug dealer. The fact that Brady coached Newton's son at the local footy club might explain their interaction. She said she had told Brady of her suspicions about Newton's likely role in Krystal's disappearance on a number of occasions before the homicide squad's involvement and she said he shrugged it off, suggesting that Krystal was the one responsible for her own disappearance.

Karen said Krystal loved a party and always made a big deal of the birthdays of significant people in her life, even buying presents for the local publicans. 'She'd no sooner have her own birthday and be planning the next.'

When Krystal didn't contact the family on her brother Aaron's birthday on 18 July, Karen said that she believed there was little prospect of her returning, believing from the beginning that she was never coming home. Twelve days later, on Karen's own birthday and without any contact from Krystal, she said she accepted that she would never see her daughter again.

Despite this conviction, Karen said she has never given up hope. She has kept herself busy in the pursuit of answers by developing posters early in the piece for local awareness, establishing and maintaining the Facebook group continuously for almost twelve years, seeking advice from clairvoyants and using the media. She says the family can never put this behind them until they locate Krystal or are at least provided with some definitive answers and have the chance to say goodbye.

Karen said she had been frustrated by police telling her that Krystal's case would be the subject of a coronial inquest, declaring that she had been hearing this on a regular basis for almost eleven years. The inquest finally opened on 11 July 2022, thirteen years after Krystal's disappearance.

Karen recently stressed, 'it's not even about punishing the person that did it now, it's not even about that, I just want to know why, and where she is, I want to bring her home. If we knew where Krystal was we could relax a bit. It wouldn't make it go away but I could live with it a bit better.'

* * *

Neil Fraser said he has never been spoken to about Krystal by investigators other than the initial discussion/interrogation in 2009. He is even more surprised that no police have ever got back to his mother, Helen, who made the initial report to Jason Brady about Krystal's disappearance. He said he assumed that this would have been a priority for investigators, but despite the many changes of personnel assigned to

Krystal's case over the years, none have.

Neil said he always worried that something bad would befall Krystal because of her disability. He said his interest in moving to the bush was strengthened when Krystal, at an early age, left her parents dealing with a teller in a bank and climbed on to the knee of a man seated in the reception area. 'She thought the best of everybody,' he said.

Asked what action, if any, he took to establish what had happened to Krystal, he said, 'I didn't want to stuff it up for the police by getting involved in the investigation and I was angry. Karen and Tilly got right behind the Facebook group but I couldn't. I wanted answers, I wanted a result. That's why I spent nine years working in Melbourne afterwards, only returning home on weekends. I needed to get away from the talk and the lack of a result in the investigation. I was angry and felt that I might have done something I would regret if I hung around Pyramid.'

CHAPTER TEN

Krystal Lee Fraser

Krystal was born on 18 August 1985 in Melbourne, Karen and Neil Fraser's first child. They were living in Dandenong at the time. It was established that Krystal had experienced a foetal brain injury, cause unknown, resulting in a condition known as hydrocephalus. According to the *Oxford English Dictionary the name is made up of the Greek hydro, meaning water and the Latin cephalus, for head; hence the common term for the condition 'fluid on the brain.'*

The disorder is characterised by too much cerebrospinal fluid (CSF) inside the ventricles of a child's brain. Ventricles are spaces inside the brain where CSF is produced. The main role of CSF is to cushion the brain in the skull, acting as a shock absorber. Excess fluid increases the size of the ventricles thus putting pressure on the brain. Hydrocephalus can permanently damage the brain, causing problems with physical and mental development. Children may experience learning disabilities, behavioural impairment and physical disabilities[3].

Surgeons considered a number of options but eventually determined that surgery was not necessary for Krystal.

Karen related that, 'Krystal was hard work growing up, she annoyed the crap out of her brother and sister, frustrated them no end. But as they got older they began to empathise with her more and more and to help her. You had to be careful how you spoke to Krystal for she took everything you said quite literally, if you said it's raining cats and dogs, she would look for them in the rain.'

Krystal attended Pyramid Hill College, which consisted of junior and senior campuses, comprising prep to year six and years seven to ten. Years 11 and 12 were completed at the nearby Boort District P-12 School. Karen described Krystal as a wizard at reading and writing, saying that she never really got the opportunity to read to her because she had three kids under three. She said Krystal loved school and if she could have kept going she would have, adding, 'She loved the social side of things but her friends, sadly, were the teachers, not the other kids.'

This lack of schoolmates is underlined by comments made by Kerryn Watson, who as a young hairdresser working at Bettina's Hairdressing in Pyramid Hill regularly overheard Karen Fraser complaining that all the kids in Krystal's class were having sleepovers and Krystal was never invited. After hearing this a number of times Kerryn invited Krystal to stay with her at her place in Bendigo, which she did on several occasions.

Karen said Krystal's teachers used to tell her that Krystal struggled, saying that although she could read she didn't understand the context, or what she was reading. However, Karen said '...she had an amazing memory for numbers and of things she was interested in, such as music, movie stars and their movies.'

I asked Karen if she could recall any examples of Krystal having been treated differently from her peers as a child. She provided two that readily came to mind. 'We had a pool in the backyard and we bought special swimsuits for the kids with floaties built into them around the waist. Krystal wouldn't put her suit on and jumped into the pool whenever Neil was in there knowing he would keep her afloat. We nagged and nagged her, but she refused to put that suit on. So I encouraged Neil to keep an eye on her but let her experience the danger of jumping into deep water when you can't swim. She bobbed up and down a couple of times and afterwards let us teach her how to swim. Sometime later the woman who was running the local pool came to my door and said Krystal couldn't go to the pool anymore without adult supervision. I said, "Do you know that Krystal is over ten years old and can swim across the pool?" And when the woman agreed, I said, "Then she is allowed to attend the pool on her own and if you refuse her you will be guilty of discrimination." There was never any more trouble. Another time, one of her teachers rang and read me a story that Krystal had written at school and it contained explicit references to sex. I asked her why this was a big deal as she should know about sex at her age. But the teacher said, "It's not that so much, it's that the characters named in her story are her fellow pupils." I said, "Why couldn't you bring this up with Krystal? You are her teachers, you should have dealt with this with her." I felt that if it were another child, they would have managed a situation of this kind with the student personally.'

After completing Year 12, Krystal worked at her parents' Pyramid Hill bakery/café until they sold it, and later at the IGA supermarket in town for a while. It was rumoured that she had also began a pre-apprenticeship at Bettina's Hairdressing in Pyramid Hill. Bettina Hawken, who operated the salon for forty-five years, said Krystal spent a lot of time there but never worked for her. She said that Krystal would sit down next to her customers and say, 'My name's Krystal, what's your name?' Bettina said that she didn't see a lot of Krystal during the latter stages of her pregnancy, the last time was about two weeks before she disappeared. '…she popped in and she had a bag of veggies, and I said, "Are you having a party Krystal?" and she said, "Could be, anyway, gotta go." That's how I knew Krystal, the sort of relationship I had with her, I probably treated her like a mother.'

Bettina said that anytime she saw Krystal she would ask her if she were excited about the baby and Krystal would say, 'I can't wait to push her around the football oval. And that was because she would see young mothers doing it and it was very trendy. Krystal apparently got up to some things that shocked me. I didn't think she was capable of some of these things but obviously she was, and I am a little naïve when it comes to things like that. I felt so sorry for the poor little bugger, she was a lonely kid, had to make her own decisions and fend for herself. The baby would have been great for her and I had every confidence that she would have made a great mother.'

Karen said that 'Krystal was an amazing little girl and then she got to seven and just plateaued, was an easy-going kid until she turned eighteen, then she changed. She had been told at many government agency meetings by many people over the years that she could do whatever she wanted when she was eighteen, and she did, unfortunately.'

In Year 10 Krystal did work experience for one term at the IGA supermarket in Boort. On these days she caught the V/line bus which deposited her at the Boort railway station. On her walk from the railway station to the supermarket she would drop into the Boort police station and speak to SenConstable Ray Stomann, the town's sole police officer. Stomann said Krystal would march straight into the station and say, 'How you going? What's happening?' Adding, 'She was always friendly but not smart. She wouldn't leave unless I made up some bullshit excuse to get her out of the station.'

Krystal's official Victoria Police missing person circular remained on the wall of his police station on the day of my visit (18/08/2020). Stomann recently reflected that he would love to see this solved for Krystal's and the family's sake. He believes Krystal's family had trouble controlling her and that living with her was really frustrating for them, with her often getting out her bedroom window of a night to visit people. He said he was aware that after Krystal moved out of home she refused to take advice from her parents. He believed that their Horsham business relieved some of the stress she was putting them under, stressing, 'Don't get me wrong, the Frasers are good people, and they did everything in their power to help Krystal along the way.'

In terms of single member police station officers, SenConstable Stomann is everything that a small community would desire. He is currently in his thirty-seventh year as the officer in charge of the Boort police station. Approachable, sound, caring and supportive of his community, he is universally trusted and enjoys tremendous respect in the town where he serves on half a dozen community committees.

Both Karen and Neil Fraser referred to Krystal's sense of humour. She liked to have fun. Neil recalled that when she was about sixteen or seventeen Krystal started to call him her stepfather, which he wasn't. 'One night around this time she asked me to take her to a dance in Boort. Jokingly I said to her that I couldn't be bothered and that maybe she should ring her real father and ask him, I'm only your stepfather. Quick as a flash she said, "I would if I had his fuckin' number."'

Krystal moved out of home into her own flat, in Kelly Street, Pyramid Hill, at nineteen years of age. Karen said this had been Krystal's decision, no longer willing to comply with her parents' demands of letting the family know where she was, who she was with, being home for meals and home by a reasonable hour. Karen said she engaged social workers from Bendigo to assist Krystal with the acquisition of the flat. State Trustees were appointed to deal with Krystal's money, paying her rent and bills and drip-feeding her remaining funds into her debit card throughout the course of each fortnight. Before this Karen had been managing her finances for her but said that this had become intolerable with Krystal quite regularly screaming at her in the family's business, 'You owe me money.'

Karen said that as a result of Krystal's intellectual disability she was extremely gullible, and people took advantage of this. 'I didn't know Krystal was even having sex until we got a call from the police one night saying she had broken into a guy's place across the road and he'd come home to find an incredibly angry Krystal cooking up his dinner, despite being dumped by him. He was not a nice person. She began to knock around with more and more really awful blokes and wanted to bring them home. I kicked out the first one she brought home and told her this was never gonna happen again, he and all the others she was knocking around with were the worst kind of men.'

Krystal's pregnancy came as a shock to Karen and when Krystal first mentioned it during a phone call to her in February 2009, Karen recalls that she said, '...that's ridiculous Belle, you've got an implant in your arm that stops you from getting pregnant.' She said Krystal had insisted that she was and Karen dismissed her. Karen knew that Krystal had had a contraceptive implant inserted in her arm at the Pyramid Hill nurse's station in September 2008.

Although promoted as being 99.95 per cent effective in preventing pregnancies, research indicates that epileptic medications may stop the implant from working. Karen said Krystal was on anti-epilepsy medication at the time as a consequence of previous seizures(4). The implants, known as Implanon, take effect after seven days. It is conceivable then that Krystal became pregnant just before the implant or within a few days of the procedure, as her baby was due on 23 June 2009.

Krystal rang Karen a few days later with the same pregnancy proclamation and Karen said that she told Krystal, 'Don't be fucking stupid, I told you it is not possible, Krystal said well I've got an x-ray of my baby in my hand right now, I'm pregnant mum.'

Karen realised Krystal was obviously talking about an ultrasound image. Karen said she asked Krystal if she knew who the father was and Krystal told her that she didn't. It had been established that Krystal was already five months into her pregnancy, with the baby due in June.

Karen said following news of the pregnancy she arranged for a meeting between the Department of Human Services (DHS), Krystal and herself about three months before the baby was due. Karen said at this meeting the DHS told her and Krystal she would be allowed to keep her baby and 'if she was not coping I would become his foster-carer. I warned Krystal that in effect she would be losing the baby to me if she didn't look after it properly. Krystal assured me and the DHS that she would.'

Karen said that she and Neil were negotiating the purchase of the house next door to their own so that Krystal would be living beside them with her baby. Krystal discussed baby names with the family, telling them she liked the name Conrad. Karen said she told her she needed to think what a kid named Conrad would be called at school. Krystal then suggested a few names of men in their extended family and Karen said that the child should have its own identity and for Krystal to think about it some more.

It appears that shortly afterwards Krystal visited her neighbour, Alex O'Toole, who had delivered a son named Ryan about six months earlier. Alex said Krystal had pointed to her belly and said she was having a son too and asked her if she could also call her baby Ryan. Alex said she told her it was fine.

Describing her relationship with Krystal, Karen said, 'I loved my daughter and I miss her terribly. Frustrating yes, but this wasn't her fault, she unfortunately wasn't very smart and this put her at risk with dodgy blokes because these types hung around her. Krystal's only fear was of being alone and she was going to solve that by having a child. She hated being by herself and she hated going home to her flat to just watch tele and knit. She wanted to be with other people.'

CHAPTER ELEVEN
Krystal's Interactions

I asked Karen Fraser how motivated she believed Krystal would have been to leave hospital for a party, given her advanced pregnancy, contractions and pending delivery. Karen said the invitation would have been a strong temptation, '...because she longed to be wanted.'

Societal prejudice around intellectual disability and ideas of beauty limited Krystal's opportunities to form healthy relationships. Her intellectual disability and her disregard for appearance and dress were obviously all elements of this bias. Despite her freedom, Krystal's choices over her life were arguably further burdened by a low economic and social status, contributing to her vulnerability to abuse. The experience of segregation and rejection made her more responsive to attention and affection and consequently, at risk to predators[7].

Her sister Chantel summed this up with the observation, '...she loved attention, good and bad, she couldn't tell the difference.' Her apparent exploitation sexually and as a drug courier are proof of her risk and exposure.

Chantel said Krystal knew that the family didn't approve

of the men in her life so had chosen not to tell them about who she was seeing. 'It was hard to know if the father of Krystal's child was involved in her disappearance because Krystal kept a lot of secrets. Yes, she stopped telling us about the men in her life because we were always critical of the choices she was making, they were the fucking worst.'

A further example of the secretive nature of Krystal's life was her use of the pseudonym Kylie Wright on chat lines. She also managed to keep her drug couriering/dealing role quiet as it is not openly talked about in Pyramid Hill.

Furthermore, her relationships with a number of men are not public knowledge. Perhaps she was warned to stay quiet by these men, some of whom were married or in long-term relationships. She kept these liaisons mainly to herself. Similarly, despite her professed ignorance of the identity of the baby's father, there is her chat line statement, made to Carlo Anfuso, describing the threat made to her by the baby's father in the week before her disappearance.

It is difficult to say whether substance or alcohol abuse was a factor in Krystal's risky sexual behaviour which may well have been related to an anxiety stemming from the stigma associated with her intellectual disability. She met men in pubs, almost exclusively in situations where alcohol and drugs were around, some people suggesting she had developed a dependence over time. Jason McPherson, with whom she had a close relationship until the time of her disappearance said she was addicted to marijuana.

How much emotional fulfillment did Krystal experience from these rather impersonal casual relationships? There are suggestions that occasionally she offered sexual favours for cash or goods, or money to fund a train trip, for example. Some satisfaction may have been achieved through the process, but perhaps it was all about connection for a lonely young woman.

Karen was not aware of any drug use by Krystal but acknowledged that she drank a little, suggesting that it was about fitting in, '...she made out she drank more than she did. She couldn't drink, she would be pissed on half a can. What she did was buy a drink and sip it for a while and then sit it down somewhere and buy another one so it would seem that she was drinking along with everyone else. Her smoking was the same, she didn't do the drawback, she was so funny to watch smoking. She only did it to try to belong, to look cool but she didn't, you couldn't help laughing at her.'

Karen believed that carrying a pack of cigarettes gave Krystal an opportunity to initiate a conversation by offering a man a smoke and asking for one in return on a later occasion as a prologue to a subsequent dialogue.

Karen conceded that she found a bong on a number of occasions when she had cleaned Krystal's flat. Krystal had told her she was simply minding it for a friend who lived in the same block of flats. However, on a later occasion she said Krystal said to her, 'If you ever hear rumours about me and drugs they are not true.' Karen hadn't heard any such rumours, but when Krystal mentioned the same thing on a couple more occasions Karen said she said to her, 'You know, there's an old saying, where there's smoke there's fire. If you get caught you will go to jail, and I don't do jail visits.'

Karen said that she instantly understood that there was some substance to Krystal's potential involvement in drugs when Krystal responded with, 'That's all right mum, I'm a nuffer, they've already told me I'll just get a slap on the wrist.' Karen said she said to Krystal, 'So they are true then.' Karen said that despite the comment Krystal denied it, but she was left in no doubt that a drug dealer or dealers were using her daughter and they had drummed it into her that she could get away with it because of her intellectual disability.

Chantel said that by ceasing to share information about her partners following the family's open disapproval of her relationships, Krystal may have felt a sense of guilt over these associations. If she did experience these negative feelings this may have contributed to a greater reliance on substance use and progress towards dependence. Chantel suspected that any one of nine men could have fathered Krystal's child.

Unlike her mother, Chantel readily acknowledges that Krystal was a drug user, marijuana only, as far as she was concerned. She said Krystal had told her that she used to collect drugs from a guy in Bendigo. He was Tony Gatt who is now deceased. He was apparently eliminated as a suspect as he was in rehab at the time of her disappearance. Gatt lived in Long Gully, a Bendigo suburb.

Krystal told Chantel that she would deliver the drugs, 'marijuana,' to 'Bandy' (Allan Summers), also deceased, who lived in Barber Street, Pyramid Hill. Bandy would allegedly sell it around Pyramid Hill. He would then pay Krystal after he had sold the drugs and she would deliver the money to Gatt in Bendigo and be given more drugs to transport home. Chantel said Krystal had told her that on one occasion she spent the money owed to Gatt and he forced her to sell drugs from his home and prostitute herself to repay the debt.

The predatory people involved in drugs clearly perceived her as an easy target to fulfill their trafficking activities. This abuse may also have possibly been achieved through fear and maybe less about attention or affection following her recruitment. Her poor financial situation, potentially exacerbated by drug use, may have also contributed. Isolated as a consequence of her disability, with no genuine friends, she was attracted to those showing her attention. A good example of this is in the relationships with men that were not publicly acknowledged by them. Another is of her walking up and down outside the pub until someone she knew arrived, perhaps indicating a lack of self-confidence.

Pyramid Hill publican Debbie Demaine revealed that Krystal liked to be liked, that she liked the attention of men, and was always drawn to them. 'Krystal would do anything if she felt that the person really liked her. Anything, that's why she carried drugs for people, that's why she did those things, because she thought they were her friends.'

These abusive relationships were unlikely to have sustained her, but it seems she would do anything and everything to maintain them, craving individual contact.

Karen was confident that Krystal knew about birth control. Although Krystal had refused to discuss the matter with her, she had arranged for Chantel to provide tuition on the subject. While Krystal would discuss virtually all topics with her mother, Karen said she frequently, simply stopped talking about the men in her life. Karen was grateful that she never saw any signs of violence or witnessed any injuries possibly stemming from an assault.

While it has been established that Karen was living in rented accommodation with Neil and Chantel at the time of Krystal's disappearance, this wasn't always the case during the operation of the Horsham business. When the Frasers purchased the confectionary business in late 2007 Neil was doing the run on his own and they were running it from Pyramid Hill. Karen said this began to prove challenging for Neil as he was required to make the four-hour drive to and from Horsham before and at the end of the week as the truck had to be garaged at the confectionary supplier's premises there.

Accordingly, they took a twelve-month lease on a Horsham property in November 2008, moving there then and later making the decision to return to Pyramid Hill after they learned of Krystal's pregnancy. Although seeing Krystal on the majority of weekends, Karen admits that the family's knowledge of Krystal's relationships and activities had reduced during this period. However, Karen said that any concerns they may have had were assuaged by the fact that Krystal seemed to have settled down with the pregnancy, '... looking after herself a bit better, looking after the baby.'

Karen said it was obvious Krystal really wanted her baby, telling her mother, 'I'll have done something that Tilly (Chantel) and Frogga (Aaron) haven't done, I'll be giving you your first grandchild.' Karen summed up Krystal's desire for a baby with, 'All Krystal wanted was something that was going to love her unconditionally.'

Alex O'Toole, who had lived at 38 Kelly Street, diagonally across the street from Krystal, until just after her disappearance, said Krystal didn't have any boundaries. 'I'd come out of the shower and she'd be sitting on the couch or sitting at the table, probably a dozen times over the years. She was always friendly but after a while it could get annoying, she didn't appreciate it might upset people. In terms of her intellectual capacity, people took advantage of this.'

Alex said she always assumed Krystal's disappearance involved something sinister. 'She used to fluff off a bit, she'd fake an illness to get an ambulance to Bendigo, just to get a ride, and then discharge herself straight away. This is how she'd get herself down there if there were no trains running. That's why the CERT team were a bit hesitant about going there because it was always some illness that wasn't even there just to get a ride to Bendigo. But it wasn't in her nature to just disappear and not make contact with someone.'

Alex said that there was a great deal of commentary about Krystal's involvement in drugs. 'She would do anything to fit in so people used her to take drugs to parties,' she said. 'She felt like she was doing a good deed, look, I'm invited, I'm doing all these people a favour, it meant she was liked. They would have easily lured her on this basis.'

Alex was not aware of the identity of the father of Krystal's baby but had heard a rumour circulating at the Dingee pub, where she worked the bar, that it was Stephen Jones and that he had learned that a DNA test was planned when the baby was born. Alex reasoned that, '...because someone had to be held accountable, and he'd heard, "yes I think it is yours" and he's married. It would make sense that he was involved if he were the father and he was gonna get caught.'

Krystal had discussed having both blood and DNA tests with each of her family members on a number of occasions so that she could determine the father of her baby.

Karen had been made aware of Krystal conning a ride to Bendigo via the ambulance, but said it only happened during the pregnancy and that she rarely paid her fare on the train anyway. She said that if Krystal didn't have the funds for a fare she would simply jump on the train and hide in the toilet on board. After a while the conductors got to know her habit and would knock on the door and warn her of the dangers of riding in the toilet, Karen revealing, '...they were her friends and looked out for her, often giving her a ham and cheese croissant and a chocolate milk leftover from the buffet car.'

Family friend of the Frasers of many years, Sue Lacey, who had taken Krystal to the Boort Medical Centre to confirm her pregnancy and cleaned her flat following her disappearance, said that despite having a bit of street cred, Krystal was regularly taken advantage of. 'She just wanted to be popular, she was a lost and lonely girl,' she said.

The two women shared a regular joke when Sue was working at the local supermarket, which also functioned as a Bendigo Bank outlet, with Krystal coming in regularly to check if the State Trustees had deposited funds into her account. Sue recalls that Krystal would say, '…just checkin' to see if the fairies have been, and I would respond with, "Yeh the fairies have been today".' Sue had heard rumours about Krystal's involvement in drugs and while she had no evidence one way or the other, was troubled on the trip to Boort with Krystal when she observed that she had two mobiles with her. When she asked Krystal why she had the two phones Krystal simply deflected the question. Apparently, '…she was great at avoiding questions like this.'

Chantel suggested there was nothing shifty about this as the second phone was simply used to provide additional battery power, such was Krystal's prolific use of the phone. However, it became clear during the inquest that Krystal had two phones at the time of her disappearance, one ending in the number 054 and the other 924.

While giving evidence at the inquest into Krystal's disappearance, Karen, Neil and Chantel Fraser were each shown what purported to be a suicide note alleged to have been found by police during a search of Krystal's flat. The note read as follows:

Dear mum, dad, Frogger, Amy, Max, Sam, Till, Luke and Bub, I love you all and I'm sorry it had to end this way. I had nothing else to live for, this was the only way you could all have much better and happier lives. Good luck to you all, Love Krystal.

While each of the Frasers said they'd never seen the note before and were never given reason to suspect that Krystal may have been considering suicide, Chantel was able to clarify that it was Krystal's handwriting. She said it had to have been written before Christmas 2008 because Luke, who had been her boyfriend, and her split up then.

CHAPTER TWELVE

Why Kill?

Crime statistics suggest that the majority of women murdered in Australia are killed by a current or former intimate partner[5]. At just under eighty per cent of all murders of women, the ratio of female murder victims killed by an intimate partner is about thirty per cent higher in Australia than in the US[6]. Victoria's murder rate was far higher than the national average at the time of Krystal's disappearance, sitting at 2.6 per 100,000 in 2009.

Notwithstanding this alarming data, the risk of victimisation of those with an intellectual disability has been estimated to be between three and seven times higher, compared to the general community[7].

There are numerous motives for intimate-partner homicides; jealously being the most obvious and frequent. Motive aside, as demonstrated above, the reality is that Krystal's vulnerability was heightened as a result of her intimate relationship with multiple men and her intellectual disability. Contributing further to this amplified exposure, it has been estimated that pregnant women face twice the risk of physical abuse by an intimate partner than non-pregnant women, further exacerbating Krystal's risk[8].

Were there any signs that a relationship she was involved in may turn fatal? Any reports, public or whispered that she had been assaulted or threatened? The Fraser family weren't aware of any. Perhaps there was an emerging pattern of violence towards Krystal. Was she recorded as a victim? The subject of an intervention order? Had she left a violent relationship? The only material in existence pointing directly at an intimate partner as the perpetrator, are the comments attributed to Krystal by Carlo Anfuso, who alleged that Krystal told him in the week preceding her disappearance that she feared that the father of her baby would kill her if she gave birth.

If, and the likelihood is high; the person who killed Krystal was the father of her unborn child then a reasonable hypothesis, based on the information provided by Carlo Anfuso, is that he killed her to prevent her giving birth. Why was it so important to the killer to prevent the birth of his baby? While it was most certainly about control, his justification was most likely complex. It may have been to hide his relationship with Krystal from a spouse or partner; avert mortification over exposure of his liaison with an intellectually disabled woman; or even a means to avoid maintenance for his child.

Despite the overwhelming statistics depicted earlier concerning the prevalence of violence by an intimate partner, and the aggravated vulnerability faced by pregnant and disabled women, the killer may have had no history of violence towards Krystal. He may be a respected member of his community and not meet any of the stereotypes imagined.

Murder is an exceptional phenomenon in our community. During the ten-year period from 2010 to 2019 there was an average of 162.7 homicides a year in Victoria, that's an average of 2.6 murders for each 100,000 people. This compares with 620 assaults for each 100,000 people[9]. You are 240 times more likely to be assaulted than murdered in the state of Victoria.

If the offender's reason for killing Krystal was to continue to conceal their relationship, then the intensity of his justification must have been formidable. What could be so devastating about the exposure of his liaison with Krystal that would cause him to kill her to prevent it? Assuming the killer was married perhaps, the most compelling possible reason, conceivably more persuasive than a loss of face or ridicule, or the payment of maintenance, would be the forfeiture of assets resulting from a subsequent separation settlement. Avoiding financial loss is as credible a motive as gain.

It is assumed the killer did not have an emotional dependence or attachment to Krystal and that, from his point of view, it was purely about sex. This assumption is supported by the fact that, in the final stages of their relationship, he rang her from a public telephone box. Thus Krystal potentially had no means of contacting him as he controlled the communication transaction and, if he lived in the Leitchville area, no method of visiting him as she didn't drive and her preferred means of travel, V/line, did not service that area. Maybe 'lack of attachment' is too generous for the nature of the killer's relationship with Krystal; it seems to have been more about coercive control.

While the explanation for Krystal's death most certainly could have been to prevent a spouse or partner from learning of the infidelity and the associated consequences, the public derision anticipated because of the revelation of his relationship with a person affected by an intellectual disability may have been even more overwhelming. It is highly likely that the public stigma directed towards people with disabilities would transfer to the father of Krystal's child by way of association as a result of the revelation of his interactions with her[10]. A perceived fear of public ridicule and humiliation may have been the catalyst for his actions.

While it is important to maintain an open mind during an investigation, police will be driven by the existing evidence and the lines of enquiry it presents. On the face of the information available, it appears that Krystal's disappearance did not become significant to police until details of calls to and from Krystal's mobile phone became available. Remember the comments being attributed to Brady, the police officer in charge of Pyramid Hill police station and the member initially responsible for the investigation. This officer was quoted in the *Bendigo Advertiser* on 27 July 2009 stating, '...she is now believed to be hiding interstate.'

And on 10 August 2009, '...hiding out in New South Wales with her baby.'

The details of calls to and from Krystal's mobile phone evidently opened the minds of investigators involved in the case. Police had been using these records extensively in the investigation of crime for at least twenty years at the time of Krystal's disappearance. If her disappearance had been treated as critical from the outset these phone records would have been sought and obtained promptly. The information obtained from the telecommunications provider not only gave investigators details of Krystal's associates but also the whereabouts of the phone itself.

It was established from this that Krystal's mobile was used to search the internet at 1.30 am to 1.35 am and was switched off for the last time at 2.49 am on Sunday 21 June 2009. The phone was communicating with a cell tower located in Leitchville at the time of this last signal, denoting that the phone was in the Leitchville area. It is not known whether Krystal was still in the same location as her phone at the time.

A recent canvass of fifteen homes neighbouring the Leitchville phone box established that police conducted their own door to door appeal of the area some two months after Krystal's disappearance. It was interesting to learn that this street appeal was conducted by uniformed police from Cohuna and none of the residents I spoke to had talked to detectives involved in the case. The majority of residents spoken to reported that the phone box had little use at the time of Krystal's disappearance. Most were surprised that it remained there. While a number of those spoken to offered opinions about Krystal's disappearance none were able to reveal the identity of the mystery architect of the calls made from the phone box to Krystal.

Despite numerous appeals, the unidentified caller has never come forward, strengthening the assumption that the caller was involved in Krystal's disappearance. Was he the father of Krystal's baby? Or could there have been an entirely different scenario? Was her death more about protecting a criminal enterprise? It has been established that Krystal was transporting drugs for at least one person who, investigators believe, was connected to a larger organised group involved in drug trafficking. The father of Krystal's child could have got rid of her and the baby any time after learning of the pregnancy, so why wait until the baby was almost born?

There is some speculation that as Krystal was friendly with a police officer she may have disclosed something to him about those supplying her with drugs and he has shared this with a member of the group, either intentionally or by accident. Consequently, the theory goes, Krystal may have been identified as a liability to their business. The facts, as known, do not support this theory.

The most compelling hypothesis is that Krystal was killed to prevent the birth of her baby to prevent the revelation of the killer's intimate relationship with her as disclosure could cause a great deal of humiliation to the killer and his family.

CHAPTER THIRTEEN

Reward Inducement

The investigation into Krystal's murder, as it was clearly defined by then, went cold in 2010. The last public mention of the case was the report in the *Herald Sun of 10 June 2010 of an application for a $100,000 reward. On 23 June 2012 the Age Online mentioned the approval of the reward without providing any additional information.*

It was seven years before police next spoke to the media with the *Bendigo Advertiser running a story on 17 July 2019 headlined*, 'New lead in 2009 disappearance of Pyramid Hill woman Krystal Fraser.' Det-Acting-Insp Julian Horan, of the missing persons squad, is quoted throughout the article.

The article quoted Horan revealing, 'As a result of new information being received this year investigators have renewed a number of lines of inquiry into a person previously spoken to by police.' The report suggested police believed that Krystal's relationship with a man and her subsequent pregnancy might have caused a confrontation between Krystal and the man, leading to her disappearance and death. Horan said their focus was centred entirely on this one person.

It is hardly coincidental that this 'new' information was revealed in the same article that announced the reward for information had been boosted from $100,000 to $1 million.

Victoria Police, perhaps in the interests of consistency, or equity, resolved that all rewards for victims of the same offence be valued equally; modifying its rewards system in 2015 to set the amount of the reward offered being contingent on the statutory length of imprisonment for the crime committed.

There are currently thirty-four rewards on offer in Victoria displayed on the Victoria Police website. The reward offered for information about Krystal's disappearance is, unfortunately, still listed at up to $100,000, despite the 2019 proclamation. Only five of the thirty-four rewards listed relate to the disappearance of (missing) persons.

During the decade between January 1999 and January 2009, Victoria Police did not pay out a single reward[11]. There were seven reward payouts totalling $300,000 in New South Wales in 2018: $60,000 in 2017 and none during 2014–2016[12]. There are currently 117 rewards on offer in NSW, totalling $31.5 million which, based on the lack of success they provided during 2014–2018, appear unlikely to deliver an outcome into these unsolved major crimes.

The positive nature of rewards is that they can rekindle public interest in a crime, potentially stimulating new leads or providing someone with the motivation to become involved when previously, through fear or otherwise, they did not.

Extreme or absolute fear of the perpetrator will, however, undoubtedly not change the actions of a potential source. No amount of money is worth your life. That is why it is disappointing that the reward in Krystal's case is still listed as $100,000, instead of the $1 million proffered at the media event. The former is not to be sneezed at but a million dollars is a life changing sum.

As an experienced police investigator, I found that rewards were welcome in the following circumstances:

i. When the investigation has hit a brick wall and all known avenues of enquiry have been pursued and exhausted.
ii. When there is a known offender/strong suspect, but a significant piece of evidence is lacking.
iii. When there are multiple offenders where each has played a different role and only one or some of the co-offenders was involved in the most serious aspect.
iv. When an alibi witness, who was close to the offender and provided a false water-tight alibi several years ago, may have a changed relationship now.

- In situations ii), iii) and iv) investigators will do a fair amount of cage-rattling around the time of the reward's announcement to stimulate conversations and will undoubtedly have launched electronic surveillance in advance.

Chapter Thirteen   Reward Inducement

There are inherent risks in using a co-offender who has become a witness against the main player/s purely to receive a reward. Let's face it, they were involved in the crime in the first place, they are crooks and generally have criminal histories. Defence barristers will target such histories during cross-examination to discredit them. These witnesses will undoubtedly attempt to limit their own role in the crime while conceivably embellishing the actions taken by the defendant. Furthermore, because of the witness's history, their co-offenders facing trial will know intimate details about their other nefarious activities that the informer may be very reluctant to declare. Denying other wrongdoings will put the informer in a tenuous position because the indemnity they have been provided with in exchange for their evidence, will only apply to the crime they are obliged to testify about. The indemnity will not protect them against prosecution for other crimes and they remain subject to perjury charges if they are found to be lying under oath.

When faced with questions that are likely to discredit them, they may choose to exercise their lawful right to silence and self-incrimination. The value of the witness is compromised at this point one way or the other. If they admit to other crimes, they are branded a career criminal by the defence and face the prospect of further charges. If they exercise their legal privilege to keep their mouth shut the value of their evidence against their co-offenders is diminished, often irreparably.

What often occurs at this point, and I experienced it

several times during my policing career, is that the witness (informer) begins to seriously question the decision to give evidence against their co-offender and they clam up completely, refusing even to answer the presiding judge's questions. If the case relies heavily on this person's evidence, as it clearly does if the case could not proceed before this evidence was unearthed, then the case is effectively stuffed.

The context of Krystal's disappearance may only be known to one individual, the offender. If this is the case then a reward is meaningless. However, there may exist evidence of suspicious behaviour, or confirmation of relationships, or verification of the use of a public telephone at unusual hours by a man that had a mobile phone at his disposal. It would be assumed that this type of subtle evidence should have emerged at the time of Krystal's disappearance.

Another reason to question the value of rewards is that large rewards in major murder investigations are known to create false and unhelpful information which creates a major worthless workload for investigators.

A review by the Los Angeles News Group of 372 rewards offered in that city from January 2008 to April 2013 for information to solve serious crime found that only fifteen of the rewards were paid out[12]. At 4.03 per cent this is double England's statistics but can hardly be regarded as successful. This raises the question of whether the resources applied to administering and providing rewards might be better used for investigative tools and investigators.

CHAPTER FOURTEEN

Jason McPherson

There were a number of men acquainted with Krystal who were treated as suspects or persons of interest in relation to her disappearance. Jason McPherson, who has already been mentioned, was one of these men.

I spoke to Jason via the phone a number of times in July, August and October 2020. He acknowledged a former friendship with Krystal. At the time of our discussions, he was forty years of age, in remission from bowel cancer and existing on a disability support pension. He has computer expertise and previous experience working in computer shops in rural and regional Victoria. He conceded many years of illicit drug abuse with a dependence to heroin and ecstasy. He told me his use of heroin and alcohol together was a highlight as each drug evidently heightened the effect of the other. He said he has since weaned himself off all illicit drugs as a consequence of his illness and by going cold turkey.

He said he first met Krystal when she was about fifteen or sixteen, saying that she would wag school and catch the train to Bendigo and go to a place there called the Cruiser

Bar, '...a hang-out for teenagers, which the council eventually closed because so many kids were wagging school to go there.'

Karen Fraser disputes this, saying that Krystal loved school and even went when she was sick, adding that she could never have wagged school to travel to Bendigo as the only way she could get there and back was by train, and the return train arrived back in Pyramid Hill at 9.30 pm.

McPherson said they continued to run into one another on the train over the years and they later began a relationship in 2008. He described Krystal as, '...good fun, always in a good mood and trying to make everyone happy, even when you could tell she was a bit down herself. Although she was twenty-three, she was like a twelve-year-old in a lot of ways.'

He told me their relationship lasted for about three months, ending roughly twelve months before Krystal's disappearance. Although he had his own place in Kerang, he said he would take the twenty-nine-minute train journey to Pyramid Hill every second day or so and spend the night with Krystal. He said he broke it off with her when he found out she had had sex with five or six other guys during this period. A rather mercenary attitude given that he was also in a long-term relationship with another woman during this time.

He said he was told of Krystal's infidelity by a friend who had been one of those concerned, the friend telling Jason that he had not been aware of his relationship with Krystal. He said he confronted Krystal with this accusation and she openly admitted it. Subsequently, he said they agreed to remain 'best friends with benefits' and occasionally had sex afterwards. He said that Krystal had told him after this that she loved getting with men and was happy to tell him who she was having sex with, '…she was keen for it. She was basically prostituting herself at times, not like she was standing on a street corner but like she would offer sex for stuff, even stuff from shops and money for the train.'

He said that at one point Krystal made the remark, 'I'm shagging the local piggy.' He also alleged that Krystal told him that she continued to have a relationship with Brady during her pregnancy. This claim is unsubstantiated and vigorously denied by Jason Brady. I asked Brady in May 2021 about the allegation that he had had a sexual relationship with Krystal. He said, 'Absolute bullshit. I couldn't stand being in the same room with her because of her stink. I wouldn't risk being in a room alone with her anyway because of who she was and what people might say. There was a sign put up by the previous officer at the station to prevent people going beyond the front counter. It was put up because of Krystal as apparently she used to walk right in all the time.'

The alleged statement attributed to Krystal in relation to Jason Brady should be viewed with suspicion as Krystal's family and acquaintances have acknowledged that she was prone to fabricating or embellishing stories and in light of Jason McPherson's other unsubstantiated claims.

Despite the changed circumstances of their relationship, McPherson said that he continued to be a regular visitor to Krystal's flat, allegedly buying cannabis from her and smoking it with her. He said Krystal told him that 'Twiggy' (Craig Newton) supplied her with drugs to sell, which he said she told him she did locally but mainly in Bendigo. There is no evidence to support the allegation made against Newton.

McPherson claimed that Brady and 'Twiggy' were friends but, again, there is no substantiation of this. He also said Krystal was hooked on grass and sold it to maintain a supply. He said he was aware that Krystal supplied drugs to one of the men he claimed she visited on her last night in Pyramid Hill, the night of her disappearance. He said that he often saw him when he visited Krystal's flat. He didn't identify this man.

He said the last conversation he had with Krystal was via the phone at around 9.00 — 9.30 pm on the night of 20 June 2009 when he assumed she was ringing from the Bendigo Hospital. However, it has been established that she made the call to his house from the last house she was known to have visited in Pyramid Hill that night, Robert Glennie's house. McPherson said that during this call Krystal asked him to come over the next day to fix her computer, install Windows on it. Homicide investigators confirmed this call, telling the Frasers that McPherson was at home in Kerang during this conversation.

McPherson also said that Craig Newton came on the scene with Krystal after him. 'Twiggy was married and lived in Cohuna with his wife and a number of kids.'

He said that he continued to visit Krystal on a regular basis despite her new relationship with 'Twiggy'. He also said Krystal told him that she was having a baby and that 'Twiggy' was the father of her child. He said he was at Krystal's flat on a couple of occasions when 'Twiggy' turned up and rather than leave he would stay to annoy 'Twiggy', '...who would just give me a threatening stare.'

McPherson claimed that '...on these occasions 'Twiggy' would bring dope to her, both for her own use but mainly to sell. She was putting it on tick and built up quite a debt with him. She was running the drugs on the train to repay him.' Again, there is no evidence to support any of these claims.

McPherson suggested that the relationship between Krystal and Newton ended about two months before her disappearance. He said Krystal told him that one of the reasons she had broken up with 'Twiggy' was because he wouldn't return a key to her flat. He further alleged that Krystal told him that she liked to have other visitors there and didn't want 'Twiggy' barging in on her. If this is true, then Krystal's contact with Carlo Anfuso deep into her pregnancy supports the timing of this and the reality of the proposition.

McPherson admitted that he was surprised Krystal had given Newton a key because he (McPherson) was never trusted with one. The relationship between Newton and Krystal apparently turned sour after Krystal ended it. McPherson alleged that he was at Krystal's flat a number of times when Newton had rung Krystal and, 'had given her a hard time. Krystal would hang up on him and twenty minutes later he would pull up across the road from her flat in his blue Ford sedan. He would just park there with the lights on, trying to scare her.'

McPherson alleged that Newton stalked Krystal for a while like this. He said he believed that the drug dealing between them ended along with their relationship and he was not aware if Krystal still had a drug debt to Newton at the time of her disappearance.

McPherson said he continued to visit Krystal right up to the time preceding her disappearance. He helped her prepare her flat for the new baby and shopped with her for nursery items. Although judgmental of her numerous relationships with other men he considered Krystal his friend.

* * *

McPherson said he first learned of Krystal's disappearance via Facebook. He had been expecting to hear back from her on 21 June 2009 over the repairs to her computer following their conversation the previous evening.

He said three weeks after Krystal's disappearance he moved into the house next door to the Leitchville Post Office, 19 Findlay Avenue, Leitchville. He said he often saw Newton pull up and use the phone box at the front of the post office after he moved there.

I know the property and it provided an unobstructed view

from the front of the house to the phone box, which was situated just outside the boundary of his property. He said he later informed detectives of his observations.

He said he never went into Krystal's flat after her disappearance but looked through the windows a number of times. He suggested 'Twiggy' may have entered and destroyed evidence as he had a key to Krystal's flat. Again, there is no corroboration of this.

McPherson informed me he was arrested as a suspect in Krystal's disappearance by police from Cohuna shortly after his move to Leitchville. He said that several months later the homicide squad also interviewed him as a suspect in a formal recorded interview. He said, 'My partner, Deb, alibied me and my phone logs supported her alibi as I had been home in Kerang and I'd also rung my father during the night from there.'

He further said that a few years after Krystal's disappearance he ran into Newton after his daughter Jasmine had been killed in an accident and maliciously said to him, 'I'm glad your daughter was killed because you killed Krystal, you cunt.' Jason said he assumed that Newton would fight him, '...but he just walked away.'

McPherson said he had been spoken to by a series of crime squad detectives over the years, including as recently as 2019 and 2017. He said he has never been eliminated as a suspect. While he had time to travel from Kerang to Pyramid Hill after his phone call with Krystal on the night of her disappearance, it is reasonable to assume that investigators would have been able to establish that he remained in Kerang that night. According to Karen Fraser, Krystal had told her that she wanted Jason McPherson to be godfather to her baby. Maybe he was the friend he claims he was.

During the inquest, evidence was given by homicide squad member Wayne Woltsche that he had received information that the person seen walking from the train station on the night of Krystal's disappearance by Nick Dingfelder may have been McPherson. This was based on statements made by staff at the Pyramid Hill café who had seen McPherson and Krystal in the shop together previously and believed he may have been the one with her on this particular night. Woltsche concluded that the staff were confused about dates and that Krystal never attended the café that night.

The fact that Krystal rang McPherson on his landline at Kerang less than thirty minutes later from Glennie's house and the apparent admonishment delivered by Krystal over his failure to 'fix' her computer clearly illustrates that he was not in Pyramid Hill when the train arrived there that night.

Although Jason McPherson freely acknowledged a sexual relationship with Krystal on the occasions I spoke to him, he denied it at the inquest.

CHAPTER FIFTEEN

Investigation Hiatus

As stated previously, Krystal's disappearance failed to generate any major media interest or exposure. With the exception of the recently concluded inquest and the application for and endorsement of the $100,000 between 2010 and 2012, the most recent reporting in the case was the raising of the reward to $1 million on 17 July 2019. During this disclosure, the details of a promising new lead were reported. Essentially this was the only new material, excluding reward information, since coverage of the six-month anniversary of her disappearance on 19 December 2009, some ten years earlier.

The press conference of 17 July 2019 was conducted at the Bendigo police station. The police spokesperson was Det-Acting-Insp. Julian Horan of the missing persons squad. He was reported as stating that 'Police have refocused their investigations in light of new information received earlier this year. As a result of this new information investigators have renewed a number of lines of inquiry into a person previously spoken to by police. The information is promising. However, it sadly leads us to look at the possibility that Krystal met with foul play because of the intimate relationship she shared with a man.'

While the nature of this new information was not shared, its foundation is basically indistinguishable from that acknowledged by homicide investigators ten years earlier. The Fraser family were not given details about the substance of this latest information nor the identity of the person concerned and when Karen mentioned the name 'Twiggy,' they denied it.

Notwithstanding this, the family were later informed that the missing persons squad had travelled to Port Macquarie in New South Wales to interview Craig 'Twiggy' Newton again over the matter.

Karen Fraser said Det-Sen-Constable Damon Abby, of the missing persons squad, told the family he was part of a special four-person team formed to look exclusively at Krystal's case. He told her that '(Det-Sgt) Woltsche was fixated on Peter Jenkinson and we have another good suspect.' Karen thought Abby's comments were disrespectful and said she was quick to defend Woltsche, telling Abby, 'Wayne has been great to me; without him I would have gone over the edge.'

Karen said she questioned Abby's comments because she had been made aware by homicide investigators years earlier that there were hundreds of calls between Peter Jenkinson and Krystal and at the same time that calls from his personal devices ended, calls originating from the Leitchville phone box began. Furthermore, she recalled that investigators informed the family that Jenkinson's mobile phone was detected in the area at the times of these calls.

However, not much significance can be attributed to this as the nearest telco tower to his property in Gunbower was the one at Leitchville, which also encompassed the phone box area. Karen said she believed the ending of the calls between them and the alternate means of communications via the public phone was not a coincidence. Karen suggested Jenkinson decided at that time to get rid of Krystal, and the use of the phone box was designed to hide their relationship before taking action.

Karen said that Woltsche was always of the view that Jenkinson killed Krystal because he was, or believed he was, the father of her unborn child. She dismissed this premise by saying that he had had four months to kill her, so why wait until three days before the birth to do so? She further argued that '...if some sheila that you've been having a bit on the side with comes up to you and says I'm having your baby, what do you say? Prove it. You cannot be forced to provide a DNA sample for paternity testing. You've got to think, all these people into drugs, you've got to simplify your thinking and it doesn't make sense to me. What were they going to achieve by killing her and the baby? Her saying the baby was his, big friggin' deal, it's not something you kill over.'

Karen said that Woltsche had maintained that Jenkinson had a partner at the time and because he had already had to pay out a woman from an earlier relationship, this was motivation enough.

I spoke to Jenkinson's former partner a couple of times in late 2020 and she confirmed that Jenkinson had paid her a settlement of around $100,000 following the breakdown of their relationship several years earlier. Karen reasoned that because Jenkinson's affair with Krystal had been so secretive all he had to do was, '...deny, deny, deny, and that would have been the end of it.'

Karen believes, 'Krystal was in the wrong place at the wrong time and saw something she shouldn't have, she was a weak link. That makes more sense to me than killing her because she was pregnant. He, they, had time and opportunity for some time, they needed to shut her up, it has to have been drug related.'

Chantel's explanation for Krystal's death corresponds with her mother's, believing that it was to silence her, '...she knew too much, was shagging a cop and no-one could guarantee her silence, she was killed to protect them. Jason Brady, a pisshead, got drunk and mentioned something that Krystal had said to him about someone involved and this got back to that person or persons who killed her to stop her talking.'

Woltsche's belief in Jenkinson's guilt was obviously enriched by a partial admission he alleged Jenkinson made after being released following his interrogation over Krystal's disappearance. The alleged subjective admission picked up by an unauthorised bug installed in Jenkinson's vehicle has, of course, never previously been made public. Karen said the family was advised by homicide squad officers of 'the admission' detected by the illicit listening device in her lounge room.

Karen said that she and Neil, their children Chantel and Aaron, two family friends and Aaron's girlfriend Jamie were present during this conversation with Woltsche. Karen said they were told by Woltsche that Jenkinson was detected on the bug saying, 'fuck they got me,' which was allegedly followed by, 'nah, fuck it, they won't get me.'

Woltsche's assessment of these statements as an admission has to be acknowledged. There can be no other reasonable interpretation given the environment in which they were made. If the bug was deployed, as suggested, can it be justified? Obtaining a search warrant to install and monitor surveillance equipment is demanding and is, for a particularly good reason, an onerous task. This is not a case of the end justifying the means but rather appears to have been an exercise in futility. A major opportunity lost. Is it a further example of the lack of enterprise in this case? More on the bug later.

Reporting of the 2019 media forum also referenced the arrest of a 61-year-old Pyramid Hill man over the matter towards the end of the previous year. It advised that he had since been eliminated from the enquiry. Karen Fraser said this man was Allen Summers, known as Bandy. Karen believes that Krystal visited Bandy after getting off the train in Pyramid Hill on the last day she was seen. Chantel has described Bandy as one of Krystal's boyfriends and dope clients. Karen describes him as, 'a drunk, a dirty old fart who took advantage of Krystal, but I never saw or heard of him being mean to her.'

Karen also said that Detective Abby told her that his crew had arrested Bandy because the original investigators had overlooked him and he had never been ruled out. Karen reckons, 'Bandy had cancer and was in a pretty bad way by the time Krystal disappeared. If he knew anything he would have mentioned it at the time.'

She was told that he'd been very drunk the night Krystal visited him and had little recollection, even at the time of her disappearance. Karen believes that Bandy was arrested '...so the police could go to the media and look like they were doing something, maybe hoping to shed new light on the case, but it was just hollow.'

Dressed for swimming; Krystal aged 5

Christmas morning: Krystal aged five

Happy on a Harley: Krystal, aged eleven

Me and my dog: Krystal age eleven

From left: Jason Brady and Krystal at her twenty-first birthday

Krystal and her father, Neil, at her twenty-first birthday

Krystal clebrating her twenty-first birthday with her mum, Karen

How the Herald Sun announced the $1million reward

Pyramid Hill railway station

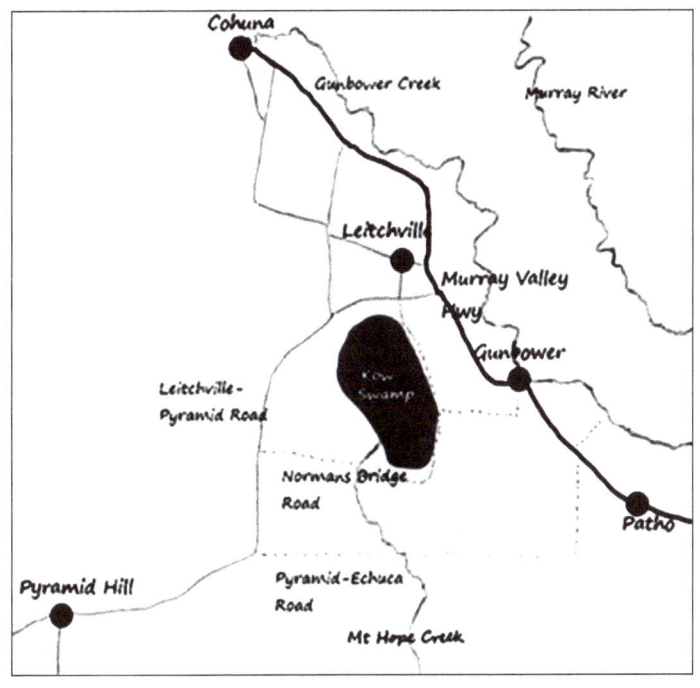

Map of locations concerned in Krystal's disappearance.

Pyramid Hill: a standout feature in the Victorian landscape, where Krystal met her lovers.

CHAPTER SIXTEEN

Stephen Hugh Jones (Deceased)

Steve Jones was employed as a truck driver by the McGillivray abattoir at Gunbower at the time of Krystal's disappearance. Starting in 2006, he delivered meat from the abattoir to butcher shops throughout the region. He moved into a rental farmhouse on Gunbower Island near the abattoir with his two teenage children around November 2008, following separation from his wife, Denise Jones. Despite the separation they remained close, Denise having moved to nearby Cohuna, and his children spent time at her home as well as with Steve. Denise was not their mother.

Steve had a variety of jobs throughout his working life. He had been a prison officer for a number of years and at some point he had held a crowd controller's licence, bouncing at licensed premises and large public events. He was busted working in this capacity at the Gunbower Cup after the expiration of his security licence.

Denise gave evidence at the inquest into Krystal's suspected death. Her statement was obtained by missing persons officers on 4 March 2022. Why was a statement not obtained by homicide squad officers during their investigation in 2009? She said that Steve and Peter Jenkinson were close friends; in fact, it was Jenkinson's property that he had moved into with his children. The property was only a short distance from Jenkinson's own hobby farm. She told the inquest that Steven and Peter Jenkinson had been friends for a long time, before she had even met Steve. It was established during the inquest that the two men had shared an interest in shooting, racehorses, dogs and cock fighting.

Denise told the inquest that a couple of years before Krystal's disappearance Steve arrived home with Peter Jenkinson and said he'd met 'Pete's new girlfriend,' saying that Krystal from the café in Pyramid Hill had told him Pete was her boyfriend. Denise said that this was about two years before Krystal's disappearance. She said, 'Pete laughed it off and denied it.' She didn't become aware of Krystal's disappearance until after Steve and Jenkinson were interviewed by the homicide squad in Echuca in relation to it.

Following Steve's police interview, believed to have been on 16 September 2009, Denise said he told her that Jenkinson had admitted to him he had been having an affair with Krystal for several years. He told her that Jenkinson had told him because it was in his interview and knew that Steve would eventually find out. Denise further said Steve was very annoyed as he had been dragged into something because of it and had known nothing about it.

As far as Denise was concerned Steve never spoke to

Chapter Sixteen   Stephen Hugh Jones (Deceased)

Jenkinson again. She further stated that she was at Steve's place in Gunbower one day after this when Jenkinson drove into the property with his girlfriend, Nguyen, and their baby and Steve had pointed a shotgun at his vehicle and ordered him off the property.

It has not been established why Steve Jones was considered a suspect in relation to Krystal's disappearance but it may have simply been on the basis of his association with her revealed by their phone communications. It could also have been as a result of his association with Jenkinson who, by this stage, because of telephone records, had become a major suspect, and Jones was being used to verify or refute specifics provided by Jenkinson. Whatever the case, Jones and Jenkinson were released without charge.

* * *

It was mentioned previously that a property in McRae Road, Pyramid Hill, was searched during the investigation with speculation in the media that there'd been two tipoffs that Krystal's body was hidden there. The fact is that when Jones' arrest as a suspect became public knowledge, Roy MeHarry, the manager of the McRae Road property contacted investigators.

I spoke to Roy in November 2020 in the nursing home where he now resides. He told me he advised police that Jones and another unknown Gunbower man had been regular shooters on the property up until the time of Krystal's disappearance and that he had not seen them since. He said that homicide detectives with around thirty emergency services personnel turned up and searched the entire area opposite the house paddock, an area which included a rocky outcrop of about one and a half square kilometres.

A backhoe was also brought on to the property to dig out a pit in which dead stock were disposed of. Nothing was found to indicate that Krystal had been at the property. MeHarry recalled that Jones and the other man had been at the property in June of that year as he was pleased to have them there before the lambing season as there had been foxes about and his attempts to bait them was no longer proving effective. MeHarry and others told me that shortly after Jones' arrest the homicide squad spent time in Gunbower speaking to people.

* * *

Karen and Chantel Fraser encouraged me to speak to a Sue McGillivray of Gunbower as they had received reports over the years that she had information about Krystal's disappearance. The Frasers were reluctant to be seen in Gunbower because Peter Jenkinson lived there. Sue McGillivray, who was operating a café in the town and had previously owned the Gunbower roadhouse, told me when I spoke to her in September 2020 that she had provided homicide investigators with information about the case years earlier.

Chapter Sixteen   Stephen Hugh Jones (Deceased)

Sue said that the day after details of Krystal's disappearance became public, before there was any police activity in the area in relation to it, Jones and Peter Jenkinson had an intense argument in front of the diesel bowser at her business. Although she couldn't hear what they were saying she said that '...arms were flying about and their body language was that they were having a big disagreement. They were yelling at each other and both were very angry.' She also said that Jones and Jenkinson had been very close before this and Jenkinson was a regular customer at the roadhouse up until that point, when he '...abruptly stopped coming in.'

She said that following the departure of the homicide squad from the area, Steve Jones arrived at the roadhouse and made a written statement to her and her daughter. While she was unable to locate it for me at the time, she found it later and it was produced at the recent inquest.

The wording of the Steve Jones document is, 'Steve Jones wrote at 3.37 pm on 23/09/2009. I Steve Hugh Jones, told the gorgeous Amy and her mother Sue that I told the head of Parana task force that if they didn't get someone — preferably Sharon or Nick — to my residence at 90 Dickenson Road (off Gum Lagoon Road) now I would kill Peter Mathew Jenkinson.'

It is notable that this occurred a few days after Jones and Jenkinson had been arrested and interviewed in relation to Krystal's disappearance. Sue said that Jones named Peter Jenkinson as Krystal's murderer but didn't provide any other information. Sue said that Jones asked them to read and countersign his document, which they did, adding that Jones was crying and upset when he is alleged to have said to them, 'I told him, not the baby Peter, not the baby.'

Asked by Sue why he was telling them this, Jones is alleged to have said, 'You are a good person, you'll do the right thing with this information.' Sue said she made a copy of the note and promptly handed it to the local police member Sen-Constable Chris Goyne. Wayne Woltsche of the homicide squad acknowledged receipt of it.

Sue said that a couple of months after this Jones, who was a regular customer at the roadhouse, arrived at their premises and asked her to follow him to his vehicle. Jones is alleged to have produced a green cotton supermarket shopping bag and upon opening it said, 'This is the shirt.' Sue said she thought she was looking at a black oily rag and said as much. Jones is alleged to have said, 'That's the shirt Krystal Fraser was wearing when she was killed, that's blood, not oil.'

He had pulled the shirt out of the bag and indicated three holes in the front of it and said, 'They are stab marks.' Jones maintained possession of the shirt and left. Although concerned for her own safety, Sue said she contacted Chris Goyne again and advised him to collect the shirt from Jones.

During his evidence at the inquest, Woltsche said that he couldn't recall ever seeing any clothing but did visit Steve Jones on the back of the information, adding, '...but clearly if he had produced something believed to be clothing, or relevant to the inquiry, it would have been seized.'

* * *

Mark Ariens, a senior constable stationed at Cohuna police station was working alone in the divisional van on 27 May 2010, eleven months after Krystal's disappearance, when he received a radio message to attend a possible suicide by shooting north of the town. Unlike most rural police officers of this rank Ariens had served as a detective for a number of years before his transfer to Cohuna. He responded immediately, arriving at the scene in the early afternoon. He instantly recognised Steve Jones, whom he had seen around town. Jones was prone on the ground with a wound to his stomach and a shotgun alongside. Jones was obviously dead.

Ariens determined that the body had not been there for long. The scene was a couple of hundred metres off the Murray Valley Highway on the banks of the Pyramid Creek, several kilometres north of Cohuna. A small navy blue four-wheel-drive with a canopy on the back was parked nearby and Ariens was aware that Jones drove this vehicle.

When Ariens called in the details he was advised by the radio operator that Jones was a POI (person of interest) in Krystal's homicide investigation. Ariens said he was familiar with the case and surprised that this information had not been shared with his office previously. Reasonably satisfied that Jones' death was as a result of the man's own hand he said he was slightly hesitant in making that judgement because there were three holes in Jones' shirt. However, while it looked a little unusual, he believed it was plausible that the shirt material had been pushed up as the deceased pressed the gun into himself, but this detail obliged him to call the responsible criminal investigation unit. Two detectives from Swan Hill attended 'reluctantly' as a result of his insistence. He remained while they conducted, '...a thorough job, appropriate in the circumstances.'

While every case of death by firearm must be treated on an individual basis, with investigators looking into the circumstances and history of the victim, an examination of the evidence available at the scene is the most critical aspect of the investigation. Investigators need to be mindful of blood spatter and evidence of contact staining. Blood patterns, which involve the sciences of physics or geometry, are the work of experts.

For example, is there evidence that the gun was pressed against the victim's stomach at the moment of impact? Were there blood stains on the firearm or the victim's hands and arms to indicate that he was holding the firearm when it was fired? Were his hands 'bagged' for the purposes of examining them for gunshot residue - tiny particles of gunpowder discharged when a cartridge is ignited? Was a crime scene unit requested to conduct these examinations?

Numerous studies have been conducted into deaths involving firearms. There is strong empirical evidence that the head is the most common site of gunshot wounds in suicides in men. With shotgun wounds to the head, it is 7.6 times more likely that the wound is the result of suicide rather than homicide and, critically, for wounds to other areas of the body the reverse is true[13]. A recent review tabled in the *American Journal of Forensic Medicine and Pathology* of 406 suicides involving guns revealed that eighty-two per cent of male suicides were the result of wounds to the head and ninety-two per cent of these occurred indoors[14]. When both these statistics are considered, the context of Steve Jones' death being a suicide could be questioned.

Ariens visited Jones' estranged wife's property in Cohuna to inform her of his death. He said there was a suicide note left at Jones' house but he can't recall its contents. However, Sue McGillivray, was allegedly told the note instructed the family to pay Jones' outstanding fuel bill at her roadhouse.

Ariens' enquiries about the shotgun found at the scene revealed it was registered to a third party from Melbourne, a person known to Jones. Jones did not possess a shooter's licence and clearly should not have had the gun. However, investigating officers found nothing to indicate that his death was anything other than a suicide, the request to pay an outstanding bill the clearest validation of this.

It is understood that Steve Jones battled with an underlying mental health issue for many years and was on pain medication at the time of his death. While the reason for his death is unknown, there were several possible contributing factors. These included stress over the unproven death of his friend Krystal Fraser; his determination to obtain evidence against a possible perpetrator; the breakdown of his marriage, chronic pain or simply being openly considered a suspect in Krystal's death.

* * *

Sue McGillivray said that immediately after Jones' death Peter Jenkinson again became a regular at her business.

She described Jenkinson as a friend, '...a good person who did something bad.' She believed Steve Jones was obsessed with trying to find evidence to prove that Jenkinson had killed Krystal. She was initially surprised when Jenkinson was nominated as a suspect but became less so as rumours about his alleged involvement began circulating within the tiny Gunbower community.

As cited earlier, Jones' suspected involvement in Krystal's disappearance was described by Wayne Woltsche as a red herring in the investigation. But maybe it is this deduction that was the red herring as it appears to have been a miscalculation.

Does Jones' alleged statement concerning the baby, ('I told him, not the baby Peter, not the baby') and his capacity to recover the shirt claimed to have been worn by Krystal at the time of her death, afford evidence of his complicity in the crime or merely reflect his determination to gather evidence against the alleged offender?

A strong resolve is one thing and there can be little doubt that the police involved in the investigation and the Fraser family were also single-minded in their pursuit of the truth. But neither party knew where to locate the shirt Krystal was alleged to have been wearing at the time of her murder.

If Jones had relevant and admissible evidence against Peter Jenkinson and the shirt had been worn by Krystal at the time of her death why didn't he provide investigators with a statement implicating Jenkinson? One possibility is that in order to provide direct evidence against Jenkinson he may have had to finger himself as a co-offender. But this seems improbable given the radically changed attitude Jones had towards Jenkinson following news of Krystal's disappearance.

The legitimacy of a falling out between Steve Jones and Peter Jenkinson, was reinforced by David Toll, who provided an alibi for Jenkinson over Krystal's disappearance. He said of Jones, 'Pete helped him out with his dogs. I didn't like him, didn't associate with him. Pete helped him out quite a lot, Pete helps a lot of people. And this bloke turned on him eventually. He threatened him with a gun once. Pete doesn't talk about it. He killed himself, I think because he knew the cops were on to him and they were chasing him for this bird (Krystal).'

David Toll, a retired lawyer, who acted almost exclusively in civil law proceedings in Papua New Guinea, lives on a few hectares adjacent to Kow Swamp in Gunbower.

Pyramid Hill hairdresser Bettina Hawken is alleged to

have told Karen Fraser early in the investigation that Jones was obsessed with what had happened to Krystal and was out looking for her body and evidence against the person or persons he believed were responsible for her death. Karen said she didn't know of Jones at that time. She said Bettina asked her during a later appointment if the police had contacted her in relation to Jones. Karen said she told Bettina that they hadn't and asked her if she knew why the police might be in contact with her over him. Bettina is alleged to have told her, 'He found a bloody t-shirt believed to have been Krystal's and went to the cops with it.'

Karen said that Bettina talked more about Jones and Krystal's disappearance and Karen said she said to her, 'If you know all this stuff then you need to speak to the police.' Bettina is alleged to have replied, 'Well I'm not going to.'

Karen recalls that she said, 'But Bettina, if it was your daughter and I knew stuff wouldn't you want me to talk to the police?' Karen said Bettina replied, 'It's not my daughter, is it.' Karen said she verbally abused Bettina and never returned to the salon.

It was brought to my attention that Bettina's property backed on to a suspect's property and she feared for her own children if she spoke to police. A pretty normal maternal response.

Karen said when she rang senior investigating officer Wayne Woltsche about the information she had received from Bettina about Stephen Jones and the bloodied t-shirt, he is alleged to have said of Jones, 'Oh, nah, he's just a bit strange that one.'

Karen is no wiser today whether the shirt ever existed. She has certainly never been shown one by investigators and its existence has never been acknowledged by them.

While it is true that investigators involved in serious crimes will at times keep things hidden from the public, including the grieving family, in the interests of the investigation, it is implausible that the Fraser family would not have been shown the shirt in an effort to identify or eliminate it if it was found.

CHAPTER SEVENTEEN
Craig 'Twiggy' Newton

Craig 'Twiggy' Newton has been referred to previously as a suspect in Krystal's disappearance. While investigators have provided snippets of information to the Fraser family and the media over the years, their reasons for categorising Newton as a suspect have been scant.

Jason McPherson's suggestion of Newton's involvement is untested and McPherson's acknowledged intravenous drug and alcohol dependencies at the time may have clouded his recollection of events. A good example of this is his statement about Newton stalking Krystal at her flat in his blue Ford sedan, when in fact Newton's vehicle was coloured maroon. Furthermore, McPherson has been unable to provide any direct or corroborative evidence against Newton or anyone else. Indeed, by his own admissions, Jason McPherson remains a suspect in Krystal's disappearance. Resentment that Newton may have taken his place in Krystal's bed is possibly also a motivating factor.

Despite Newton and his former partner having been separated for many years and both now having new partners,

Cathy (not her real name), his partner of eleven years, told me when interviewed in November 2020 that, although not close, they had remained on reasonable speaking terms because of their children.

Both enjoyed occasional sleepovers at their former partner's place when the children were younger. Cathy said that before Krystal's disappearance Newton, who was living in Cohuna, also often spent time in Pyramid Hill to see his three children, who were living with Cathy and her husband Wayne (not his real name).

Cathy was working at the Pyramid Hill bakery/café that the Fraser family had previously owned and saw Krystal on a regular basis in the shop. She said she found Krystal very secretive, never sharing anything personal about herself, although always keen to chat and hard to get away from. She said she often had to apologise to Krystal, telling her that she couldn't stand around and talk because she had a job to do.

Cathy said she knew that 'Twiggy' spent time with Krystal, having seen him with Krystal on a number of occasions, including together in his car. She said she was aware that they smoked marijuana together. She said that on one occasion 'Twiggy' brought Krystal to her house, telling her that Krystal had said she wanted to, '...come out and see me and say hello.' Cathy said she thought that was strange.

She was once also invited to Krystal's flat, with Krystal wanting help to learn what she needed for the baby and asking her to look at what she had already acquired for it.

Krystal explained she wanted Cathy's advice because Cathy had had so many kids.

Cathy said she asked 'Twiggy' around this time if he was sleeping with Krystal. She said he denied it, saying they were only friends, but she didn't believe him. She couldn't say for sure how long 'Twiggy' and Krystal were friends but recalls seeing his car parked outside her flat at 11.15 pm about a month before Krystal disappeared. She knew the car intimately as it had been her own for many years previously.

She said that she asked 'Twiggy' about this and he had replied that they were, '...just sharing a few cones.' Cathy said Krystal had told her previously that she smoked dope, but Cathy didn't believe this was the reason she and Newton were together, adding that they were together right up until the end (Krystal's disappearance).

Cathy said when she first learned of Krystal's disappearance she drove to Cohuna to inform 'Twiggy'. She said he didn't seem surprised, saying to her, 'Oh yeh, since when?' She said she told him she thought Krystal was last seen on the preceding Saturday.

Cathy said about a month later she and her husband moved from Pyramid Hill to a farm at Mitiamo after accepting a milking job there that included a house and Newton moved into their old premises on Gladfield South Road with his partner, Susan, and their three children.

Cathy said that 'Twiggy' was in their old house for no more

than a month before he left, catching a train to Queensland and leaving Susan and the children behind.

Cathy also said before Newton's departure from Pyramid Hill her 15-year-old-daughter with Newton and her younger children were at the Gladfield South Road property when discussion arose about the police searching a property east of town (determined to have been the MeHarry-managed farm in McRae Road, Pyramid Hill). Newton is alleged to have said '...they won't find her body there, she's not there.'

Cathy said that he kept repeating this, '...he was really weird, like he had some knowledge.' She thought it was strange that he was saying this but said she couldn't have said anything because '...he would have exploded, just gone off, you could not mention Krystal to him at all.'

She said Newton was never physically violent to her, but had been verbally cruel and she didn't dare ask him why he was saying this, adding that she had her kids with her and wanted to keep the peace. Their daughter who was present has confirmed that she overheard the remarks attributed to her father.

Cathy said on another occasion Newton was 'freaked out' because he had received a Facebook friend request from Krystal, declaring. 'how can you get a friend request from a dead person?' The friend request had to have been sent when Krystal's mobile was operational as Facebook communication is, and always has been, instantaneous.

More intriguing was Newton's acceptance of Krystal's

friendship on 5 August 2009, forty-six days after she was last seen alive and his observation that she was, 'a dead person.'

Cathy said that around this time Newton was interviewed twice by homicide detectives at the Pyramid Hill police station over the course of a week or two and she collected him from the station after each interview. He informed her that he told police during the interview he was with their son Jack (not his real name), on the night of Krystal's disappearance. Cathy said, 'He wasn't with Jack that night, Jack was home with us. He's trying to use Jack as an alibi.' Jack was sixteen or seventeen at the time, she recalls.

She said Newton was angry after each interview telling her he was only a suspect because he knew Krystal and smoked dope with her and that they had nothing on him. She alleges he told her that he kept saying he didn't do it and made 'No comment' answers to their questions. Cathy said she can't understand why, if he was a friend of Krystal's and she had gone missing, he would not have wanted to help in any way he could.

She added, 'I believe 'Twiggy' knows something and it's doing his head in, that's my thoughts. He definitely knows something and he's got something over his head. He can keep a secret, but I've told him he needs to speak up for the family (the Frasers).'

Cathy said Newton had a bit to do with Steven Jones, who also lived in Cohuna, as they had both grown up in Warragul and knew each other from there. Also Steve's brother Brett and Newton had been good mates. She said she had heard Newton talking about a guy called Pete and catching up with Pete, but she didn't know who this was. She claimed to have no knowledge of drug dealing but revealed that, 'Twiggy kept me out of the drug scene because I have no filter. He knew how I felt about drugs and he never told me anything. He was secretive about it.'

She added that he didn't work and seemed to have money, but she didn't know where it came from. She had discussed this with Susan, Newton's partner at the time, and Susan had told her that she similarly had no idea about the source of his money. However neither of them raised this with Newton himself.

* * *

Cathy said she was first spoken to by detectives in relation to Krystal's disappearance following the announcement of the $1 million reward (17 July 2019). They arranged to meet her at a bakery near her rural property. She said that she told them Newton's alibi for the night of Krystal's disappearance, that he was with their son Jack, was false and that Jack was home with her that night. She said that the investigators did not take a written statement and she was unaware whether they had ever spoken to Jack. It is surprising, given her long-term relationship with Newton, that the homicide investigators involved initially, those that had arrested Newton and interviewed him on two occasions, had never spoken to her before 2019.

Shortly after her interaction with police Newton contacted Cathy and told her he had been set up by his best mate. He told her that the mate, Johnny, got him drunk and began talking about Krystal's case, once at Heyfield and again on a subsequent occasion in Warragul, in the belief that he would make admissions. Newton allegedly told her Johnny was trying to get him to confess so that he could claim the million-dollar reward. Cathy said Newton wasn't sure whether Johnny did this of his own accord or was collaborating with the police.

She said that Newton, '...did a runner and went up to Port Macquarie as a result of the attention.' This Johnny was obviously sharing information with investigators and I initially believed he was the catalyst for the revitalised investigation and Detective Acting Inspector Horan's comments at the press conference in Bendigo on 17 July 2019 regarding new information being received about a suspect previously interviewed. However, I have since learned that the source of 'the new information' was a woman from Geelong who visited an old friend in Cohuna in May 2011 where she gleaned information about Krystal's case.

The woman, Nell (not her real name), had been reluctant to become involved through fear but finally alerted police in May 2019. She told missing persons squad officers that Krystal's death was openly discussed by a group of men at her friend's house in Cohuna. She said that she eventually made a statement to investigators about this information when the secret became too much of a burden, having maintained her silence for eight years until now.

She said the officers involved, Det-Sgt Maurie Ryan and Det-Sen-Constable Benjamin Gordon, promised to show her photographs to help identify the people she described and would keep her abreast of any developments in the case. She said they didn't do either. This could have been because they had identified these individuals based on her information and there was no need to involve her further. When there was no further contact with police she decided to provide the Fraser family with her information. She declares that this was always her objective but that she couldn't locate Krystal's parents because she didn't know their names or where they lived. It was after reading an update of Krystal's case that she discovered Karen's name and tracked her down on Facebook, subsequently ringing her with her knowledge in October 2021.

Following this call, I encouraged Karen Fraser to ring investigators and provide them with the material gleaned from Nell, as the Fraser family had never been told by police of this Cohuna connection. She did so and was told that as a result of the intelligence Nell had provided, the investigation into Krystal's disappearance had refocused squarely on Craig 'Twiggy' Newton. This confirmed the family's suspicions that this was the case as Detective Abby had told the Fraser family around the time of the 2019 media conference that he had been to Port Macquarie and had reinterviewed a suspect who had previously been looked at.

Up until this time I had assumed that the 'new information' related to what Newton may have disclosed to Johnny and the exposure of his apparently false alibi on the night of Krystal's disappearance. But it now seems clear that investigators discovered something useful during their scrutiny of Nell's friend and the group of people she encountered at his house in Cohuna back in 2011. It is possible, and indeed high likely, that someone Nell had encountered at the Cohuna house had fingered Newton for Krystal's death. It also seems Newton may have divulged something of his connection with Krystal's disappearance to this Johnny for his dogged attempts to get him to confess and the missing persons squad's subsequent trip to Port Macquarie to reinterview him.

During an interview with Cathy, I asked her about the substance of the following excerpts from her Facebook which were made in 2010.

Cathy
Hello K..... I know someone who has info about krystal and she rang crimestoppers about 3 weeks ago and they told her the detectives will get back to her and still haven't? Can you let tilly know please. She might be able to get them to do something please.

Twiggy was apparently the driver of the car. He implied he was and the guy that killed her killed himself over it

K......
Eww was that the guy that shot himself???

Cathy
Yeah that was him. Steven jones

Cathy told me she can't remember this Facebook exchange but is adamant that it was never raised with her by police. She was unable to elaborate on the material contained within these posts. It is unfortunate that Cathy cannot recall or expand on the contents of these Facebook posts with her friend from the time for there can be little doubt that the narrative exposes a potential link between Newton and Krystal's disappearance, at least from Cathy's perspective.

She did recall, however, that Newton told her there was a connection between Krystal and Steven Jones and that Jones was the one who killed her because he was the father of the baby. It's perplexing that Cathy was able to recall the comments concerning Steve Jones, which align seamlessly with her Facebook posts from ten years ago, but is totally unable to explain the incriminatory reference to Newton in the post.

Cathy said that when she told Newton she was being interviewed for this book he told her he didn't want to know about it. Her reaction to me over this was, '...if you've been accused of something you'd want to clear your name, wouldn't you? I don't understand it.'

Cathy also made the following observation about the initial investigation into Krystal's disappearance. 'There was no police, no police caravan set up, there was nothing in Pyramid Hill, you would not have known that's where Krystal was from. Nothing to suggest that the police were taking it seriously.'

* * *

Chantel Fraser traced Susan, who followed Cathy in a long-term relationship with Newton, and she agreed to talk to me. She had been living with Newton and their three children, two of whom were his, in a rented house in William Street, Cohuna, from 2006 until 2009, when they then moved into the farmhouse previously occupied by Cathy and Wayne near Pyramid Hill.

She said that Newton convinced her to move on the basis that the house was bigger and the rent cheaper. However, she said that after they had moved in she felt Newton wanted her there to isolate her even more as it was seven kilometres out of town and she didn't drive. She was completely reliant on Newton, saying, 'He wore me down, destroyed my confidence and basically treated me as his doormat, our relationship being pretty shit from the word go.'

Susan alleged that Newton wouldn't let her wear makeup

and she wasn't allowed to wear certain clothes. She claimed he often spent his entire pay (government benefits) at the pub in one day so that she couldn't have any. 'Nine nights out of ten he wouldn't be home when I went to bed and I wouldn't know where he was. He didn't come home at all some nights. He liked to stick his dick wherever he could.' She also said that she could never get near his phone, 'he would go right off if I tried.' She described Newton as an alcoholic and dope abuser.

She said she suspected both before and after Krystal's disappearance that Newton was having a sexual relationship with her, but he had denied this. She would see Krystal at the football in Pyramid Hill, where Newton's son Jack played, sometimes sitting and chatting with her. Krystal reminded her of '...a puppy dog that was lost, she was obviously lonely.' Susan said Newton told her that he and Krystal had a drink together sometimes, he gave her a lift occasionally and went to her place '...for a few bongs.'

She said Newton refused to discuss Krystal's disappearance with her, but recalled him saying a few times that they would never find her. After police interviewed him she asked him what had happened and he told her if she wanted to know anything she could watch the tape of the interview. She said she did and, 'I learned he was fucking Cheryl ....., from Cohuna, he admitted it on the tape.'

Susan said that she believed Newton had used her as an alibi and she made a statement originally supporting him but after viewing receipts from a shopping trip to BigW in

Bendigo she contacted police and made a new statement, withdrawing the alibi and told police she wasn't able to say if he was home or not.

She said she was a little vague about the timing because she'd had a severe virus just before Krystal's disappearance. Asked if Newton's son Jack was living with them at that time, Susan said that he spent time with them and with his mother and had been living with Newton and her for a while but felt that at the time of Krystal's disappearance, '...he was only visiting and not staying after his father got the shits with him and sent him back to mum's.'

Susan said Newton left for Queensland after being interviewed by the homicide squad, '...he left me stranded, seven fucking k's out of town, with kids and no licence, he just fucked off saying he needed a break.' She said that he had initially told her he was going to join mates there and would be back in two weeks, but the period of his absence kept increasing and he ultimately assured her that he would be home for her birthday on 31st January, but he wasn't.

While he was away, during the school year, Susan said she had to walk her children, aged six, nine and ten, seven kilometres to school, '...until one of my neighbours took pity on us and started picking us up.' Newton hadn't returned after almost four months, when Susan said he eventually contacted her and convinced her that he had obtained a home in Brisbane for them all to live in. After establishing his address, Susan said he never told her where he was before this; she travelled there with the children on the train and put their furniture on a truck.

Susan said when she arrived in Queensland she discovered Newton didn't have a house at all. 'We spent the first week there in a tent in a caravan park until his mate John (Crane) felt sorry for us and let us sleep in his garage.' She said that shortly after this, 'Twiggy belted my son so hard across the head that it echoed around the room, my son didn't say a word, I didn't see it, just heard it. But I could see my son's distress. I confronted 'Twiggy' and he denied it. He then started abusing my son for dobbing him in and I had a go at him telling him that my son hadn't said anything.' She said that Newton screamed so loudly that everyone in the house heard it, yelling, 'I don't want them here, I don't want to be their dad anymore.'

Susan said that Newton expected her to argue but she recalled that she calmly said, 'You have said everything that needs to be said, there is nothing left for me to say.' She said Newton got up and started throwing everything around the room and then walked out. She returned to Victoria a couple of days later with her children, her relationship with Newton finished.

Asked about the maroon Ford sedan Newton was driving at the time of Krystal's disappearance Susan said, '...he banged it up chasing Cheryl in a road rage incident. Don't know what happened, but he left our place in a real flip and came back with the car all damaged. It wasn't long after this that the car went. I'm assuming he either sold it or got rid of it. I have no idea where it went.' Susan said the police never asked her about the car, she didn't believe it was ever examined by them as it was well gone by the time they arrived.

The only occasion Susan recalled Newton coming home to the Cohuna house in a mess was one night when he was involved in a fight in the Cohuna pub. She said it was one or two in the morning, his t-shirt was ripped and he had blood down the side of his neck and on his t-shirt, one ear was ripped. 'Twiggy had a big mouth and big attitude. He acted tough and scary but was a coward when it came to dealing with the fallout. He would bluff if threatened or he was drunk. But he would fight if necessary, even if he couldn't win.'

Newton's former partner Cathy and her husband Wayne backed up Newton's account of these injuries being sustained in a fight at the Cohuna pub as Newton had rung Wayne and asked him to travel across from Pyramid Hill to help him deal with his assailants. Wayne confirmed that he did so, fronting up and making enquiries at the pub, learning that two footballers had taken to Newton and had since left.

CHAPTER EIGHTEEN
Sting Operation Targeting Newton

I was keen to speak to John Crane (not his correct name), referred to as Johnny earlier, after learning from Newton's former partner Cathy that he had tried to get Newton to confess to Krystal's disappearance. Chantel discovered his details and I had a lengthy conversation with him in February 2021 as he was eager to talk.

He told me he was an interstate truck driver. He said Craig 'Twiggy' Newton contacted him in late 2008 or early 2009. The two men had been friends for years, Crane growing up in Morwell and Newton in nearby Churchill in the coal mining region of the Latrobe Valley of Victoria. He recalled that Newton told him he was staying in a caravan park in Pyramid Hill at the time but shared a house with his partner, Susan, in Cohuna. Keen to catch up with Newton, Crane said he asked him if there were any events or functions suitable for children happening in the area, telling him that he and his family would travel there for a weekend if there was. Soon afterwards Crane, his wife Di, and some of their six children and another family travelled to Pyramid Hill planning to stay at the caravan park and catch up with Newton.

Unable to stay at the caravan park they stayed the first night at a motel in nearby Cohuna. The following morning Newton visited them there and took them to his home. They all attended a local show on the Saturday and the visitors stayed another night. (The annual Cohuna Agricultural Show was held on Friday 20 and Saturday 21 March in 2009). Crane's group returned home to Gippsland the following day.

A couple of months later Crane said he received a phone call from Newton who told him he was ringing from a phone box in Pyramid Hill. During the call he said Newton asked him, 'Can you talk to my new missus and tell her how many kids you have because she doesn't believe me.'

Crane said that he told Newton he already knew Susan and Newton said, 'Not Susan, I'm not with her anymore, I've got a new girl and she's having our baby. I'll put her on.'

Crane said a woman came on the line and said, 'Hi, my name is Krystal, I'm having Craig's baby.' Crane said she told him that they were down the local pub playing darts or pool and it was a Thursday or Friday night. Crane said he told her that he had thirteen or fourteen kids, he couldn't recall how many he'd had at that time. He later told me that he has twenty children. Crane said that the phone went dead and a couple of minutes later he got a phone call from a mobile he didn't recognise. It was Newton again who said, 'This is Krystal's phone.'

Crane said he asked him why he'd used the phone box when he had her phone and Newton told him there were too many people in the pub. Crane's wife said she also spoke to Krystal to congratulate her, saving Krystal's phone number into her phone.

Crane said that a week or two after this conversation he saw news of Krystal's disappearance on television and attempted to contact Newton via his mobile without success. He said that he also got a call from Cathy, Newton's previous partner. He said she said to him, 'Something's wrong with Twiggy, he's gone off the rails, he's gone stupid.'

Crane said he told her that he had only been talking to 'Twiggy' and his new girl a week or two before and Cathy had said, 'Oh, you know he was with Krystal.' He said he told her the details of his recent phone conversation with Newton and Krystal.

Concerned by Cathy's comments in relation to Newton's behaviour and the welfare of Krystal and her baby, Crane said he rang Crimestoppers in Melbourne, telling them about his conversation with Newton and Krystal, and the context of the call. He said he was told that homicide investigators would get back to him in relation to this information. Crane said he made this call in 2009, shortly after Krystal's disappearance, and received a call from the missing persons squad in response to this information about ten years later. He said there was no other contact with police during the intervening period.

Crane was living in Port Macquarie when he received this call from police but had lived in Queensland for a number of years before that. He said a detective told him that they had been looking for him since 2009. He said he told them this was bullshit because they were ringing the same phone number he had used when he made the call to Crime Stoppers and that he had had that number since 2007. He said he was asked if he was still prepared to speak to them about the information he had supplied to Crimestoppers and he consented. Members of the Melbourne-based missing persons squad arrived at his Port Macquarie front door less than twenty-four hours later. Crane believed this occurred in June 2019. He said the investigators asked him if he was prepared to meet with Newton and attempt to get a confession out of him in relation to Krystal while wearing a wire.

Crane said he agreed to do so with a couple of conditions. Namely, that he take two of his mates with him and that they travel to Victoria on their Harleys. He said the police officers told him that they were all the back-up he needed but Crane told them that his mates worked differently from the cops and he preferred their company.

While the use of an accommodating member of the public in a sting operation is a legitimate course of action it is not considered best practice in covert policing. The conventional methodology is to use a member of the public known to the target only for the purposes of an introduction of an undercover operative, an experienced police officer trained in clandestine policing and chosen on the basis of the target and their environment. The best acknowledged case of such an operation involved the outstanding deception committed on the suspect in the disappearance of Daniel Morcombe, the thirteeen-year-old who was abducted from a bus stop on the Sunshine Coast, Queensland in December 2003.

This is not the place to provide a detailed description of how undercover police operate, but what clearly separates them from amateurs is their ability to adapt, deflect and innovate. Such traits are developed through extensive training and experience and guided by trained covert controllers, almost exclusively sergeants or senior sergeants. The two detectives handling Crane were senior constables, not supervising personnel, so I'm guessing they were not trained covert controllers.

Another issue that may arise from using a member of the public known to the suspect is that they may find themselves having to discuss their own, previously unknown criminality with the suspect, while recording the conversation. This can result in the target becoming suspicious when the other person refuses to discuss it or says something ridiculous in response. It can also lead to the destruction or contamination of the recording by the person engaged to assist the police.

Despite the ten-year delay in acting on Crane's intelligence the police operation moved rapidly, with Crane and his mates travelling to Victoria within two weeks of his first meeting with investigators. Crane said on his arrival in Gippsland he rang Newton and arranged to catch up with him the following day at his home in Heyfield. Crane and his mates travelled from a nearby regional city with missing persons squad officers following in their vehicle. A few kilometres from Heyfield, Crane said the convoy halted while police fitted a digital recording device to his body. The police remained in this location while the other three continued to Newton's.

It is difficult to comprehend why the police allowed the other two to accompany Crane. In the simplest of terms, it would have meant that all three had to be collectively briefed on the purpose of the operation and provided with cover stories, including background so that no-one said anything that might reveal their true role and jeopardise the operation. Furthermore, they were unnecessarily exposed to covert policing methodology and technology. They were clearly superfluous to the operation and were not necessary to provide a cover story for Crane as his long-term friendship with Newton was clearly sufficient.

Crane recounted that he and Newton spent time alone in the house while the other two, along with Newton's then partner, Georgina, and several mates that Newton had called around were drinking in the backyard. Crane said Newton invited him inside 'for a chat' and upon entering the property Newton immediately turned the music up very loud. Crane said he told Newton he was having trouble hearing him, but Newton refused to turn the music down while they talked.

He said that in an effort to calm Newton, Crane began talking about drugs. Newton quickly closed this avenue of discussion saying he didn't touch drugs anymore, only alcohol. Newton began talking about Cathy and their kids and Crane said he asked Newton, 'What about that other girl you had. That girl on TV?' He said Newtown said, 'Yeh, it's over ten years and now it's an historical case.'

Crane said he asked, 'That was your missus?' Newton responded with, 'Yeh, yeh.' Crane said he asked him what had happened to her and Newton changed the topic away from Krystal. Crane said his attempts to get him back on track failed.

Crane said he suggested that they join the rest of the party in the backyard and Newton had said, 'Nah, stay here for a bit, there's something I've got to tell you mate.' Pressed by Crane to elaborate, Newton allegedly said, 'No-one knows, I moved here because no-one knows my background, so when we go outside don't mention her.'

Crane said he told him, 'I didn't even know her, mate, I spoke to her on the phone, mate.' Crane said Newton then asked a number of questions about the two blokes travelling with Crane, possibly a little apprehensive. Crane said that Newton said, 'I really need to talk to you about something.' Crane said he arranged with Newton to meet him at his mother's place the following day. He said he gave Newton $200 to help ensure he made the trip. The two men apparently joined the others in the backyard drinking for another couple of hours and the three men left on their Harleys and met the police at the rendezvous point a short time later.

Crane said the cops returned to Melbourne planning to return when he advised them of the time of his meeting with Newton the following day.

If Newton and Georgina had discussed the day after the others had all left and found the dialogue of the three visitors didn't all gel, the operation could've ended before it bore any fruit. Unnecessary risks to the success of the operation were taken by involving Crane's cronies.

Crane said the next morning Newton rang him and said he was fifteen minutes away. Crane said he rang the investigators who told him they were still forty-five minutes away. Crane said they told him that as he had to be fitted with a wire again, he would have to stall Newton. He said he then organised with Newton to meet him in a nearby park. Police fitted the wire to Crane again before he and his wife, and a couple of their kids, who had also travelled to Gippsland in a truck, met Newton and Georgina at the park.

They were all sitting around when Georgina is alleged to have said to Newton, 'Now's the time Craig. You wanted to talk to John, I got everyone outside yesterday and you didn't do it. Now's the time. Tell him what you want to tell him and ask him what you want to ask.'

Crane said with that the women and children left to buy lunch and Newton said, 'It's just so hard to get your head around it, no-one understands.' Newton is alleged to have then talked about no longer speaking to Cathy and Susan, previous partners and mothers of his children, and Crane said he asked him why this was and Newtown had said, 'Long story, all the shit that went down in Pyramid Hill.'

Crane then asked him what he wanted to talk to him about and Newton is alleged to have said, 'I need help. You know what it's like to keep a secret.' Despite spending much of the day together Crane said there was no more conversation of this nature. He arranged to meet Newton at a motel in another Gippsland town later that night. He then had the recording device removed by the detectives.

Crane's crew and Newton and his partner met at the motel later and spent time drinking together. At around 10.30 pm Crane said Newton asked for his address in Port Macquarie and borrowed a thousand dollars from him, providing no explanation for wanting the money. The following day Crane said he tried to contact both Newton and Georgina all day without success.

The next day he said he received a phone call from his mother-in-law who told him that Newton and his partner were at his place in Port Macquarie. His mother-in-law put Newton on the phone and Newton said they had decided to move up there. Newton allegedly adding that they hadn't taken anything with them, telling Crane that they had left directly from the motel, not even returning to their flat in Heyfield.

Crane said he asked him why and Newton replied, 'I had

to get away, man, it's too close, it was on the news. Ten years to the day. A historical thing, too close, too close, I had to go.'

Crane said he asked Newton about his phone and was told that he had thrown it out the window. Asked why, Newton allegedly said, 'Too close, it's too close.' Crane said that he had also seen the announcement of the ten-year anniversary of Krystal's disappearance. Newton, who was advised by Crane that he was heading back home, is said to have asked him to find somewhere private for them to have a talk when he returned to Port Macquarie.

Crane said he advised the police officers involved in the case of the planned meeting with Newton and they promptly flew from Melbourne to Port Macquarie and again fitted Crane with a wire upon his arrival there at about 8.30 the following morning. Crane said he arranged with a mate to 'borrow' his house for the day and took Newton there. He said they talked about Cathy and their kids for a while and then Newton allegedly said, 'You know no-one will ever find Krystal where she is. They will never find her. No-one.'

Crane said he asked him what he was on about and Newton said, 'She was put in the truck, in the meat mincer.'

Queried by Crane, he said, 'That truck drove from the knackery. They won't find her, ever, no-one.'

Crane said he mentioned the fact Krystal had been pregnant and Newton responded with, 'Yeah she was about to have a baby.'

Crane said he told Newton he didn't think he could be

charged over the baby as it hadn't been born and Newton said, 'Oh I don't know, mate, but they'll never find her, but remember years ago we had that saying that whatever happens we don't talk about it and we take it to the grave, well it just plays on my mind man.'

Crane said he asked Newton what he was talking about and Newton had replied, 'I don't know how to deal with it and the hardest thing is I see it on the news all the time and when I see it I fuckin' go off.' Crane said he asked Newton, 'Did you do it?' and Newton said, 'Yeh, yeh, no worries, everyone says I killed her, everyone says I did this, I did that. Well, I was with Jack.'

I have established that Jack Newton, Cathy and Newton's son, was sixteen years old when Krystal was last seen in 2009. Crane said he told Newton that he hadn't seen Jack since he was young and Newton allegedly said, 'Yeh, he was with me.' Crane said he queried this and Newton said, 'I was in the knackery and I was waiting for the truck to come in and I was saying to one of the people there how long until the last truck comes. Jack came to meet me and asked me why I was so dirty. I told him that I'd just been helping the boys at the knackery put the fuckin' stuff in the truck.' Newton allegedly also told Crane that when he got home that night Susan also asked him why he was so dirty, suggesting he'd fallen over drunk and he told her that he had.

Crane said Newton then asked him if he would like to ring Jack. Crane said he did, asking Jack if he could tell him what was going on (referencing Krystal's disappearance). Jack Newton is alleged to have said to Crane, 'Is dad telling you that I was with him?' Crane said he acknowledged this and Jack replied, 'I was not with him at all. I swear to God man, I was not with him, when he came home he was dirty as. Dad drinks a lot now and we don't speak. I haven't spoken to him for a hell of a long time.'

I contacted Jack Newton for comment in relation to the matters raised by Crane but he angrily declined to answer any questions, most concerned about where I'd got his phone number.

the, but?' to which Newton replied, 'I don't know where to start.'

When I asked Crane if he ever asked Newton why Krystal was killed, he said, 'Twiggy wanted a baby but didn't want a baby. And it's on the tape where he said that Krystal was intellectually disabled and he didn't want to have a baby with a disability. That would be the hardest thing to bring up. I can't deal with that.'

Crane didn't elaborate on Newton's arrest and interview by Victorian detectives in Port Macquarie and when I asked him if he knew what information police had put to Newton during their interrogation, considering this was a rearrest, he was unable to reveal anything.

When I suggested the police would have put the admissions he had obtained via the wire he'd worn, he was ambivalent, even naïve, saying, 'Twiggy didn't have anything with him when he left the cop shop.'

I asked him how his relationship with Newton had been since his arrest, to which he replied, 'I can ring Twiggy anytime, he considers me his mate still.'

I advised Crane that Newton's family members were saying that Newton had told them that Crane had tried to set him up, that Newton had referred to him as a 'rat.' Crane's response was, 'He's guessing. The cops told me they would be able to keep me out of it.'

The foregoing material and quotations involving Crane are all based on what he has provided and are grounded entirely on his integrity and memory of his conversations with Newton. The transcribed recordings of the conversations between the two men have not been made public by investigators. However, if Crane's recollection of the dialogue between Newton and himself is accurate, it seems incongruous that Newton was not charged.

The unconfirmed recorded disclosures attributed to Newton by Crane, if verified, provide direct evidence linking him to Krystal's disappearance and are supported by several pieces of circumstantial evidence. However, the indirect or circumstantial evidence furnished to validate a case against Newton, can also be interpreted differently, countering the assumptions made:

Aspect	Corroboratory	Exculpatory
Knowledge	His remarks about police not finding Krystal's body in an area being searched and that it would never be found. Statement about Krystal being disposed of in a truck and a meat mincer. Comment in relation to receiving a Facebook friend request from a dead person.	Simply repeating comments overheard and not from his own knowledge. Merely 'big-noting.' Or repeating gossip overheard. A statement of fact and by the time he accepted the request it was recognised that Krystal was presumed dead.

Aspect	Corroboratory	Exculpatory
False Alibi	Alibi that he was at home in Cohuna with his son on the night of Krystal's disappearance fabricated.	Had no proof of his whereabouts, or couldn't even remember, so created the alibi to avoid suspicion given his recent association with Krystal.
Opportunity	Knowledge & relationship with Krystal. Juxtaposition of their relationship and Krystal's pregnancy. His lifestyle & environment of alcohol and drug dependency. Freedom of movement. No accountability to his partner.	He was one of many suitors at the time. Several of the men in Krystal's life exhibited a similar demeanour and experienced comparable levels of independence and lack of accountability.
Means	Owner of a vehicle and a mobile phone.	Too commonplace to genuinely consider.
Capacity	Larger and stronger. Known for pub fighting. Emotional & economic instability. Previous partners describe him as verbally and emotionally abusive.	No reported instances of violence against Krystal or any other women.

Aspect	Corroboratory	Exculpatory
State of Mind	Phone conversation between the Cranes & Krystal within a week or two of her disappearance in which Krystal's pregnancy and his paternity is celebrated.	Prospective influence/ partiality of John Crane.
Post Offence Conduct	Behaviour suggesting a consciousness of guilt:- His false accusation against Steve Jones.	False accusation not made to authorities, again simply repeating something he overheard as there were many also naming Steve Jones as the father and the killer.
	Abruptly travelling to Qld without his family following the second homicide squad interview. Leaving Heyfield, abandoning all his possessions & disposing of his phone after media coverage of the tenth anniversary. Seeking $50K for a new identity & to abscond overseas to avoid missing persons squad interview.	His flight initially from Pyramid Hill and later Heyfield and his intention to leave the country could all have been attributable to the pressure he felt he was under, innocent and unable to demonstrate it.

Aspect	Corroboratory	Exculpatory
	Destroy evidence of his paternity and any ensuing financial responsibility.	His mental state may have also been a factor
Motive	Evidence of Carlo Anfuso that the father of her baby had threatened to kill her. Aware of Krystal's disability affecting the baby.	Fathering children to a variety of women of little consequence to him.

Were Newton's actions related to the crime or some other matter? The recurrent avoidance behaviour and the timing of each suggests his conduct may have been related to his culpability. The most significant characteristic of this indirect evidence is the false alibi he provided; a reasonable premise is that the truth of his whereabouts on the night of 20 June 2009 may have implicated him in the crime. The false accusation levelled against Steven Jones that he was the killer is also telling.

The fact that Newton was not charged by the missing persons squad on the basis of the admissions attributed to him by Crane, implies that the disclosures may not have been as compelling as Crane had asserted. Without knowing the true context (and wording) of the exchanges between Crane and Newton, the most serious of the 'admissions' made relates to the following statement, 'She was put in the truck, in the meat mincer.'

Newton is not alleged to have said that *he* put Krystal in either the truck or the meat mincer. He does acknowledge, if Crane is to be believed, that he was present on the basis of, 'That truck drove from the knackery.' But again, in fairness to Newton, it could be argued that he was simply repeating something he had overheard.

His alleged comment about having trouble living with the memory is more revealing about his state of mind but is less than what is required to constitute an admission of guilt. The 'memory' referenced may simply have been about his failed marriages and strained relationships with some of his children, and not about Krystal.

Crane's integrity, however, is supported by the fact that he did supply intelligence in relation to his suspicions against Newton to Crimestoppers some ten years earlier.

My recent attempt to interview Newton was rejected by him with the following comment, 'I am completely innocent and if you mention my name in your book you will be sued. You are listening to a person that can only see a million dollars and I don't want anything to do with it. I was cleared ten years ago but all these people see is dollars and they think they know it all.'

I have since spoken to Det-Senior Constable Brett Thexton of the missing persons squad who took over the lead investigator's role from Detective Damon Abby when the latter was transferred to the homicide squad. I had been informed earlier that Thexton was compiling an inquest brief

Chapter Nineteen Covert Operation Aftermath

in relation to Krystal for the coroner and I had provided him with updates previously about the results of my research.

Thexton rang me immediately after my brief phone conversation with Newton. Newton had complained to him that he was still being considered a suspect. Thexton was annoyed with me and told me so. I mentioned the extensive investigation he had been involved in using Crane and during which he had clearly considered Newton a genuine suspect.

While being careful of the language used, Thexton gave me the impression that Crane was unreliable. As far as Newton being considered a suspect he said, 'Halfway through the interview with him in Port Macquarie I knew he was innocent, he is no longer a suspect.'

I then asked him what the focus of his squad's investigation into Krystal's disappearance had been since clearing Newton. He replied, 'We are only focused on one man now.'

When I asked him if that was Peter Jenkinson he neither confirmed nor denied, simply repeating, 'One man only.'

I told him my inquiries led me to believe that Jenkinson was responsible for Krystal's murder, emphasising the homicide squad's corresponding position. I briefly mentioned developments concerning the alibi provided by David Toll for Jenkinson and the evidence I'd gleaned from Shannon Jones, Steve Jones' daughter.

Thexton was dismissive, saying, '...we have spoken to her and already have her statement, and Toll's evidence is insignificant...,' before hanging up. I was surprised by his comment concerning Shannon as I had never been informed by the Fraser family that she had provided a statement, the contents of which clearly put Peter Jenkinson in the frame for Krystal's murder.

I address the topic of Brett Thexton and Shannon Jones later in what became a dramatic development in the investigation into Krystal Fraser's disappearance.

CHAPTER TWENTY

Peter Jenkinson – 'PJ'

Peter Jenkinson, widely known simply as 'Pete', has lived in the Gunbower area all his life. He grew up on the family dairy farm a few kilometres north of town, near Leitchville. He was born in 1969 and has five siblings, including an identical twin brother. He is a skilled cattleman and although afflicted with Crohn's disease, maintains a high level of fitness and has done so for many years.

He describes himself on his Facebook page as being single and lives on a twenty-five-acre block on Gunbower Island. He works in the livestock industry as an employee and also as a private contractor performing artificial insemination, dehorning and freeze branding of cattle. He is acknowledged as a diligent worker and is well respected in his field. It is not known if he was in a relationship at the time of Krystal's disappearance but if he was it is understood that they lived independent of one another.

It has already been established that Jenkinson had to pay a former partner around $100,000 following their separation some years beforehand and homicide investigators believed this, and the fact that he was paying child support for another child, was a strong motive for him to want Krystal and her baby out of the way. While this might sound contentious given that his potential paternity of Krystal's baby could not have been confirmed without DNA testing, which he would have been unlikely to consent to, the Family Law Act establishes that a person is the biological father of a child if he is named as the father on the birth certificate[15]. So, it would have been immaterial whether he provided a DNA sample or not if Krystal had decided to have him formally recorded as the father on the birth certificate. Similarly, to claim the government baby bonus which Krystal was fully aware and had every intention of applying for, the father must also be named on the application.

Although courts, pursuant to the Family Law Act, can order DNA testing to determine paternity, the legislation does not provide for a person to be compelled to submit to one. The situation would change if there was sufficient evidence to put before a criminal court of Jenkinson's probable involvement in Krystal's death, and Krystal's baby or a sample taken from it during the pregnancy is found for comparison. Hence the potential relevance of the geneticist's report obtained by Krystal during her pregnancy that went missing from her flat, presumably around the time of her death.

Karen and Chantel Fraser made inquiries with Detective Abby about the possibility of the results of this test still being available within health services and they say he advised them that they were not. I also prepared applications on behalf of Karen Fraser for the results of this chromosomal analysis obtained from Krystal from two major hospitals understood to have treated her during her pregnancy. Again, without success, as a record no longer existed.

Details of telephone exchanges between Peter Jenkinson and Krystal have been addressed previously, including the fact that when calls to and from one another ended, calls to Krystal's mobile from the phone box at the Leitchville Post Office began. Before the cessation of the phone calls between them, thirty-seven days before Krystal's disappearance, there were numerous calls to and from one another.

As stated previously, the Fraser family were informed by Wayne Woltsche that when Jenkinson was interviewed by members of the homicide squad in 2009, following his arrest in relation to Krystal's disappearance, he denied ever using the phone box concerned to ring Krystal. However, Woltsche told the family that Jenkinson conceded that he had rung Krystal in the week before she disappeared and that she had told him that she was in the Bendigo Hospital awaiting the birth of her baby.

Despite this admission, the Fraser family were also told by homicide investigators that there was no record of a phone call emanating from either Jenkinson's mobile or home phone to Krystal at the Bendigo Hospital during this period. They were also told that records showed that Krystal's mobile phone and the phones at the Medihotel were not the source of any communication between the pair at this time. This was confirmed by Tim Miller, a retired business specialist in the law enforcement section of Telstra who examined phone records for investigators and provided technical evidence in relation to call charge and reverse call charge records at the recent inquest. The term call charge simply refers to the fact that the calls are chargeable, that there is a cost involved.

Wayne Woltsche stated during the inquest that Telstra records show that a phone call was made from the phone box at the Leitchville Post Office at 7.45 pm on Tuesday 16 June 2009 to Krystal's mobile, while she was at the Bendigo Hospital. Tim Miller of Telstra also confirmed this. The call lasted for a duration of 182 seconds. Woltsche said Krystal made a diary entry on this day and the significant thing about the entry was that she included the date and time and gave an account of what she was doing and feeling. She had noted the time as 7.30 pm and the entry was dated 16 June 2009.

Woltsche gave evidence that it seemed like Krystal was in the process of writing and was interrupted by the incoming phone call. Krystal had written that she was in the Medihotel, was having contractions and hoped that the baby would arrive soon and then when she began writing again her writing followed a completely new theme, having composed, 'My good mate PJ just called and I could be catching up with him if I go home this weekend with any luck I'll be able to, hopefully.' Krystal had also recorded Jenkinson's mobile phone number alongside the entry.

Although Krystal noted Jenkinson's mobile number next to the entry, Telstra records show that this phone call originated from the public phone at the Leitchville Post Office and not from his mobile. Jenkinson's acknowledgement of a call to Krystal at the hospital when interviewed by homicide squad members, Krystal's explicit diary entry, and telco records revealing that the call emanated from the Leitchville phone box, all strongly suggest that he used this phone to communicate with her on this occasion. And that he falsely denied it when interviewed by investigators later.

If Jenkinson used the Leitchville phone box on this occasion, namely 7.45 pm on 16 June 2009, there is a reasonable inference, given his denials and the evidence provided by telco records which refute his statement, that he also used it to ring Krystal on 20 June, the day of her disappearance.

It might also expose the level of control Jenkinson exercised over Krystal. The fact that Krystal had abruptly ended all calls to Jenkinson some thirty-seven days before her disappearance, was pertinent, particularly given their previous cellular connection and Krystal's prolific use of her mobile in general. So, too, was her willingness to meet him in the circumstances dictated by him while maintaining secrecy of their relationship and putting herself through the ordeal on the last two days of her life, returning home in response to phone calls originating from the Leitchville phone box in an apparent effort to meet him.

Additionally, it must have been extremely challenging for

Krystal to maintain the discipline demanded by Jenkinson by not trying to contact him when it appears she was waiting to hear from him in the Pyramid Hill pub on the Friday night after leaving the hospital earlier that day. While it's true that she had no credit on her phone at this time, Krystal was well known for borrowing phones to make calls. There was also a phone box located across the road from the pub.

In all media coverage of Krystal's disappearance, investigators, including those from Bendigo CIU, homicide, missing persons, and the crime department, have all articulated the correlation between the 'mystery caller' using the Leitchville phone box and Krystal's disappearance. Wayne Woltsche of the homicide squad was cited in an *Age* article of 15 October 2009 declaring that the (unidentified) person who made the midnight call to Krystal's mobile on the day of her disappearance was the focus of their inquiries.

This conviction has endured throughout the years, with Det-Acting-Inspector Horan of the missing persons squad telling a media conference almost ten years later (on 17 July 2019), 'I believe this caller holds the answers to what happened to Krystal and may be the father of Krystal's unborn child.'

Further substantiation of Jenkinson's acknowledgement of a call to Krystal while at the Medihotel was revealed only recently by missing persons investigators when they unearthed a statement made by Sen-Constable Chris Goyne, the officer in charge of Gunbower during the period of Krystal's disappearance. Goyne, responding to a request from Sen-Constable Brady, who had apparently recovered a list of Krystal's associates from her flat, questioned Jenkinson about his knowledge of Krystal's whereabouts. This was nine days after her disappearance. Goyne, in the interests of good policing, had the foresight to make a written record of his conversation. He recorded that Jenkinson told him he had spoken to Krystal while she was waiting to give birth in the Bendigo Hospital (Medihotel) and that it was on the Thursday or Friday night of the previous week, which the two men calculated to have been 18 or 19 June 2009.

Again, there was no record of calls originating from Jenkinson's phones to Krystal on these days but there were two calls from the Leitchville phone box to Krystal's mobile on Friday 19 June 2009, one at 7.08 pm and another at 8.53 pm. The timing of this interaction is particularly important for it can be argued that the matter under discussion is proximate to the actual events, and therefore unsullied by time. Jenkinson may be able to argue that he was mistaken when he told homicide investigators, some two months after Krystal's disappearance, that he had rung Krystal while she was in the hospital, as his memory of events had faded over time. However, this rationale would simply not wash in terms of his disclosures to Chris Goyne only days after the experience.

Feedback I received since the inquest from an associate of Jenkinson is that he is telling people, 'Goyne is a lying cunt, I never told him that stuff, he is making it up.' It is worth remembering that at that early stage of the inquiry police were treating the matter as if Krystal had orchestrated her own disappearance. Goyne would clearly have not considered Jenkinson a suspect at the time, simply an associate who might assist police in tracing Krystal.

The Fraser family learned that during Jenkinson's interview by homicide detectives he provided an alibi for the night of Saturday 20 June 2009, that he was playing chess with David Toll, a friend, at Toll's Gunbower-Pyramid Hill Road property, located about 6.5 kilometres west of Gunbower, opposite Kow Swamp. The Fraser family were told by investigators at the time that Toll supported Jenkinson, having told them that Jenkinson had left before midnight and headed towards his Gunbower home as he left his place.

I discovered that Toll's property is somewhat isolated and given this and his tight relationship with Peter Jenkinson, I took my mate Bob with me when I visited him. We made an unsolicited visit, as was my practice. On our arrival, he was amiable, telling us he lived alone as his wife was in permanent high care due to a serious illness. While we were speaking to him in a courtyard at the rear of his property an unknown man walked from the house unannounced. I was glad of Bob's presence.

It turned out he was a friend of Toll's visiting for a few days. Despite this, I must admit I found myself very vulnerable at the time, appreciating I'd spent several months investigating a murder without any authority or support. To clarify, David Toll gave me no cause for alarm, it was simply that at this point I accepted that I was an old man with a malignant blood disorder encroaching in the affairs of a probable killer.

I questioned Toll about his alibi for Peter Jenkinson. He told me that he had rung police involved in the case because he'd heard that they reckoned Jenkinson had something to do with Krystal's disappearance and he knew Jenkinson could not have been involved when he learned Krystal had disappeared on a night that Jenkinson was with him. He described Jenkinson as, '...better than family, I see him more than I see anyone else, he's my best mate, have known him for almost thirty years.' He said he and Jenkinson played chess very regularly back then and recalled that on the night concerned, Jenkinson had arrived at his premises between eight and nine in the evening and left at 11.00 pm.

He said he knew that Jenkinson turned right, in the direction of his home on Gunbower Island, after leaving his driveway, '...because I went outside to have a piss and saw him.' Toll lived with his wife at the time but he told me she was in hospital receiving treatment on this particular night. He said that no-one else was at his premises that night.

Queried about the time at which Jenkinson left his premises on this night Toll was adamant that he'd left at 11.00 pm, adding, 'I knew that he had to get up at five o'clock the next morning and drive 200 kilometres, all the way to Euston, New South Wales.'

If this is true then the alibi Peter Jenkinson has relied upon is futile as it fails to safeguard him during the period that the definitive call was made to Krystal from the Leitchville phone box and her departure from her home in Pyramid Hill sometime afterwards. An undisputable detail is that the trip from Toll's premises to Leitchville, either via Jenkinson's home on Gunbower Island, or alternatively via Gunbower, would take less than thirty minutes.

The integrity of Toll's alibi for Jenkinson on the night of Krystal's disappearance is further tested by observations made by Ariee, his wife of more than twenty years. Ariee Toll, since deceased, was a beautiful Papuan woman, a former flight attendant who remained bright and cheerful despite living in fulltime care, stricken with kidney disease. She migrated to Australia from New Guinea in 1996 and on to the farm at Gunbower with Toll in 1997. They married in 1999. She entered fulltime care in 2018 and was undergoing dialysis three times a week when I met her in February 2021 in the Cohuna District Hospital, a pleasant and compassionate rural community resource.

Asked about the night that Krystal disappeared, she said she was at home that night. 'I stayed out of that, not involved in it at all, I don't know what happened and how it started. It was something between them (Toll and Jenkinson) that I never got involved with. I stayed out of it because it wasn't my place to get involved with it. So I stayed out of it and I didn't even ask for the reasons and whatever.'

I advised her that her husband had told me only very recently that she was not at home that night as she had been in hospital receiving tests. She responded with, 'No, I wasn't, I was there, I don't know why David would say that. I was there but I never got involved in it. I remember that night and that's it. I vacated myself to my room to leave them alone. I cannot say anything about it because I'll get involved.'

Asked if she knew what time Jenkinson left her house on the night of Krystal's disappearance, she said, 'I have no idea; I was in bed.'

I asked her if there was ever any discussion about Krystal's disappearance between her husband and herself she said, 'No, I stayed out of it. I didn't want to get involved by them telling me about it. I stayed away from things like that because I didn't want to get involved.'

Ariee told me she had never been spoken to by investigators in relation to Krystal and when asked if she was aware that her husband had provided an alibi for Jenkinson, she said, 'No, I never asked questions. But I didn't know he had gone to the police; no, I didn't know that.'

When I queried her about this she said, 'That particular thing I stay out of it because that's something to do with the men.' I then asked her if it could have involved anything sinister and she said, 'Could be, and I didn't want to get involved, I'm sorry.'

Asked when she first became aware of Krystal's disappearance, Ariee said, 'They (Jenkinson and Toll) were talking about it, I heard, yeh, but I didn't want to be involved in it because then I knew I would be in for whatever questions they asked. Actually, I heard on the news, but the talk, which was it, I didn't want to involve myself in it. For a lot of the time, I sort of stayed out of that problem because I know he (Jenkinson) was involved with a lady being killed, whatever their situation was before she died and that I don't know.'

I have quoted Ariee precisely here and this statement could be erroneously interpreted that she was saying that Jenkinson was involved with a lady (Krystal) being killed, but this was not Ariee's meaning, she was simply saying that Jenkinson was involved with a lady and the lady was killed.

I asked Ariee if she believed Krystal's disappearance presented a problem for Jenkinson and her husband. She replied, 'Well, that's their problem to solve. When I heard about it I stayed right out of it because it is no good getting in the middle and getting yourself into a situation that you can't get out of.'

There was an underlying caution and nervousness in Ariee's words. She gave me the impression of someone who may have battled with her suspicions and a willingness to scrutinise them. And while her recollections of that night support the alibi provided by her husband for Jenkinson in terms of his presence there, she clearly could not offer an approximation of the time that Jenkinson left their property as she had 'vacated' to her room upon his arrival. There are several noteworthy issues stemming from the comments she made:

- Investigators appear to have failed to test the alibi provided for Jenkinson by David Toll by speaking

to Ariee (if Toll lied about his wife not being present on the night of Krystal's disappearance the inference surely is that he may have also lied about another aspect of the alibi).
- Toll never discussed his alibi for Jenkinson with Ariee (in fact she said that she never knew he had provided one).
- Ariee was aware that there was a connection between Krystal and Jenkinson as she had overheard Jenkinson and her husband speaking about it.
- Ariee chose not to ask questions or involve herself in the matter, conceivably out of suspicion of Jenkinson and her husband.

David Toll told me that he spent most of his legal career involved in civil litigation. However, he would have been fully acquainted with the value of an alibi in a criminal matter. While it is accepted that the credibility of an alibi witness who is an acknowledged 'best mate' of the accused will generally not be as reliable as an independent one, Toll's status and tenure as a lawyer could potentially have overwhelmed any reservations. Did this have a bearing on the decision of investigators not to pursue the legitimacy of the alibi?

According to information provided to the Fraser family by investigators, Jenkinson was not able to provide any corroboration of his whereabouts later in the night or for the early hours of 21 June 2009.

Homicide squad investigators must have suspected that

Jenkinson was their man to have established an illegal clandestine listening device in his vehicle either during the course of his interrogation or immediately beforehand. What is not known about the 'admission' Jenkinson is alleged to have made subsequent to his interview is whether it was recorded. If it was not recorded it could never be presented in evidence against him. However, despite the apparent breach of the Surveillance Devices Act (1999), if the illegally obtained evidence (Jenkinson's partial admission) was recorded, then it is likely it would not be excluded by a court exercising its discretion under the Common Law rules of evidence[16].

On the other hand, illegally obtained evidence provided by intercepted telecommunications (phone taps), is rendered inadmissible by section 77 of the Telecommunications (Interceptions) Act (1979 Cth), courts having no discretion to include them. No such proscription exists within the Surveillance Devices Act (1999).

As mentioned previously, it has been alleged that Krystal's encounters with Jenkinson took place in secret at the picnic area at the base of the summit walk at 'the hill,' off the Pyramid Hill-Leitchville Road, east of town. Krystal would respond to a phone call from Jenkinson and walk to an unknown point to meet him before travelling in his vehicle to the picnic area, and later being dropped off before walking back home.

* * *

Chapter Twenty   Peter Jenkinson — 'PJ'

Kerryn Watson, the young hairdresser referred to earlier who befriended Krystal, stayed at Krystal's flat on one occasion. She said that it was in early 2009 and that while Krystal was not aware of her pregnancy at the time, Kerryn believed she must have been. She said Krystal was always happy but on this occasion she was moody and snappy. Kerryn added that she was shocked to see Krystal smoking a bong as she hadn't been aware that Krystal used dope.

She said that while she was there Krystal received a phone call and said that she had to go and meet a guy for sex. Kerryn said she told Krystal to get the guy to visit her as she and another friend had come to visit her. Krystal told her that this guy didn't want anyone to know about him or that he was with her. She learned that the guy was ringing from Leitchville and that he was going to meet Krystal at a regular pick-up point and take her somewhere else to have sex with her in his car. Kerryn said Krystal told her that she used to do this all the time. Kerryn said that Krystal was only gone for about half an hour. Kerryn also said that Krystal told her that the bloke she was meeting for sex had a brother whom Krystal also knew.

Kerryn said she maintained a relationship with Krystal, essentially via the phone, but saw her again at Krystal's flat about two weeks before she was due to have the baby. She said Krystal told her that she had had a lot of partners and was trying to get one of these men to own up for the baby and be a father to it. Kerryn said that Krystal was in the process of writing a letter to one of these men at the time.

She recalled that Krystal told her that the guy she was writing to was from Swan Hill. Kerryn said that Krystal was sitting down to a feed of bangers and mash which Krystal told her was her lunch, Kerryn said she thought this was weird, because it was four o'clock in the afternoon. As Karen Fraser will attest, this was how Krystal rocked, she ate when she was hungry, slept when she was tired and changed her clothes when she felt like it, normal conventions were not relevant to her.

Helen Fraser, Krystal's grandmother, said that Krystal told her that she was a drug mule for Gunbower people and named 'PJ,' with whom she admitted to having a sexual relationship, telling her that the drugs involved were 'only grass.' Krystal is also said to have told her grandmother that PJ used to visit her at her flat and that she also saw him at the picnic area at 'the hill.'

Helen said Krystal was at her place on a couple of occasions when PJ had rung her and asked Krystal to go to 'the hill.' Helen said she growled at her granddaughter declaring that this was no way to be treated by a man. When discussing her drug couriering with her, Helen said that Krystal told her that PJ had told her that she could avoid getting into trouble if caught with drugs by telling police that she was a 'nuffer' and intellectually disabled.

The secretive nature of Peter Jenkinson's relationship with Krystal is best illustrated by David Toll's apparent ignorance of its existence. Toll, who had been friends with Jenkinson for many years and describes Jenkinson as his best mate, with whom he regularly played chess and smoked dope told me, 'I only learnt he knew her after she disappeared.'

While Krystal was a prolific walker, it is unlikely that she would have been able to accomplish much of a walk given the stage of her pregnancy at around midnight on 20 June 2009. She had already walked from the Pyramid Hill railway station to friends' places in Albert and Barber Streets before returning home. And while Krystal often walked the streets of Pyramid Hill 'at all hours' it is unlikely that someone wouldn't have seen her on the night of her disappearance and advised police subsequently.

Round eleven of the Loddon Valley Football League, played on Saturday 20 June 2009, was a home game for the Pyramid Hill footy club (defeating Marong by fifty points), which suggests that there should have been some traffic around midnight in town and on the route to the picnic area on the Pyramid Hill-Leitchville Road that night.

Krystal didn't visit the local pub or her grandmother on this, her final night, as she had on the previous day following her return to town, so very few people would have been aware of her subsequent return. It is worth recalling that she denied being at the Bendigo railway station when quizzed by her mother and failed to tell her that she was returning to Pyramid Hill that final night.

According to Jason McPherson, Krystal also neglected to mention that she was back home during their telephone conversation while Krystal was at Robert Glennie's place in Albert Street after her arrival back in town that night.

* * *

The local publicans, David and Debbie Demaine have both commented that Krystal was not her normal self on the Friday night in the pub — the night before her disappearance.

Present at the hotel that night was Melodee Hose, who was there with her partner Tyson who was working in the district, and their friends. She gave evidence at Krystal's inquest. She said Krystal approached her between 8.30 and 9.00 pm and '...it was obvious she wasn't quite right. She was excited about being a mum.'

During their time together she said Krystal was constantly checking her phone. 'While leaning into me like it was a bit of a secret,' Melody said Krystal told her, 'I'm waiting for my mate to call. They're coming to get me.'

Phone records show that Krystal received a call at 8.53 pm that lasted two minutes and emanated from the phone box at the Leitchville Post Office. Telco records also show that at 8.49.52 pm Peter Jenkinson's phone pinged off the Leitchville phone tower when he checked his message bank at that time.

The publicans decided at about 11.00 pm that Krystal should not be at the pub in her condition and David Demaine asked her to leave, telling her, 'Krystal it's late, it's cold and you should be in the hospital (they had already established that she had checked herself out of the hospital against the wishes of medical staff), we are worried about you and your baby.'

The Demaines have said Krystal left the pub as advised. It has been established that it was shortly after this that Krystal rang for an ambulance and was tended to by the CERT officers and subsequently conveyed by ambulance back to the Bendigo hospital.

As referenced previously, there were two calls to Krystal's mobile originating from the phone box at the Leitchville Post Office on Saturday 20 June 2009. The first, at 5.42 pm, which may have induced Krystal to depart the Bendigo hospital, ostensibly to 'attend a party' and the subsequent one, received at 11.59 pm, when it is believed she was at her flat in Pyramid Hill, the last known communication before her disappearance.

The individual who made these and the other calls to Krystal from the phone box has not come forward in response to countless public appeals, nor have they been conclusively identified.

Homicide squad detectives told the Frasers they believed the caller was Peter Jenkinson, their conviction based on the evidence afforded by Krystal's diary entries and his concession of a call to Krystal at the hospital. Krystal's diary entry of Tuesday 16 June 2009 suggests she had just heard from Jenkinson (PJ). There was also Jenkinson's admission of a call to her at the hospital that week, which he falsely declared was made from his mobile, and the proof of a call from the phone box to Krystal just before her diary entry providing the corroboration.

Who knew that Krystal would be in Pyramid Hill on Saturday 20 June 2009? Is it reasonable to assume that Peter Jenkinson knew as a consequence of his acknowledged call to her earlier in the week at the hospital? This notion is buoyed by Krystal's contemporaneous diary entry about hoping to catch up with her good mate PJ on the weekend.

The person who made the late afternoon call to Krystal while she was still at the Bendigo hospital on Saturday 20 June, supposedly inviting her to a party, and the individual who made the subsequent forty-five second phone call to her at 11.59 pm when she was at home, clearly knew exactly where she was.

Given the limited number of calls to Krystal from the phone box it can be inferred that the caller ringing during the late afternoon was the same person calling around midnight. The rationale is that he invites her 'home' to attend a party, she obviously accepts, given her departure from hospital, and he makes contact later to confirm his earlier arrangements to pick her up.

It could be argued that more than one person was using the phone box to call Krystal during that period and Peter Jenkinson only used that telephone to call Krystal on the one occasion, that is, 16 June 2009. But if that's the case, why not acknowledge it? Does he have an explanation as to why the pair stopped communicating via their phones one day and calls from the phone box began the next?

* * *

Is the fact that Peter Jenkinson's initials are PJ sufficient to identify him as the PJ known to Krystal and a person suspected of having been involved in her disappearance? Krystal's sister Chantel had known that a Peter Jenkinson and Krystal had been friends for a number of years.

She wasn't aware, however, that they were in a sexual relationship until she overheard a conversation between a man and Krystal on Krystal's phone. She said a male voice simply said, 'meet me at the hill.' Chantel said she asked Krystal what the brief conversation was about and Krystal told her that it was Peter Jenkinson, who she referred to as PJ, and that she was meeting him at the parking area at the base of the hill where they would have sex.

Chantel said she asked her why she had to meet him at the hill and Krystal told her that Jenkinson had a wife and kids in Gunbower and he didn't want anyone to see him picking her up in town. Chantel said Krystal told her that she would meet up with Jenkinson every couple of weeks and that it was always at the hill.

Chantel also said that Krystal had poor hearing and always had the volume on her phone turned right up and she heard Jenkinson ring Krystal many times with the instructions to meet him at the hill. Although she had never met Jenkinson she recognised his voice and the familiar instructions he gave to Krystal. She admitted she sometimes checked Krystal's mobile log after these calls and saw that the caller was recorded as PJ. She said that these calls were always late in the afternoon.

Evidence was given at the inquest by Tim Miller of Telstra that all the calls to Krystal from the Leitchville phone box were '...late afternoon or later.' Chantel said that homicide investigators later confirmed to the family that one of the mobiles regularly ringing Krystal belonged to Peter Jenkinson of Gunbower.

Chantel recalled one Friday morning, which she believed was in about May 2009, following her return to the family home from Horsham with her parents when Krystal had sent her a message earlier asking her to contact her when she arrived in back in town.

Chantel said she texted her as they approached Pyramid Hill and Krystal joined them at the family home shortly afterwards. Chantel said that she was on Facebook on Krystal's phone when a call arrived with PJ displayed on the screen as the caller. She said Krystal snatched the phone from her and began talking to Jenkinson, making small talk. However, Jenkinson didn't answer Krystal's questions, cutting her off saying, 'Krystal, I want to talk to you about the money you owe me.'

Chantel said she heard him ask Krystal if she could meet

Chapter Twenty   Peter Jenkinson — 'PJ'

up with him later to give him the money and Krystal said that she could. Jenkinson is alleged to have said, 'This is the last time I'm coming to get it.' After the call Chantel said she asked Krystal what the conversation was about and Krystal had told her that he owed her money. Chantel said Krystal looked frightened and she didn't believe that Jenkinson owed her money. She said Krystal left the house soon afterwards and she saw her catching a train to Bendigo at around 2.15 pm. Chantel said this was obviously unplanned as it had not been mentioned earlier and Krystal usually spent most of the weekend with the family when they were home from Horsham.

She said that Krystal must have seen her approaching the station and was trying to hide from her, only crossing the tracks to board the train at the very last moment. Chantel said it was rather comical as Krystal was unable to move quickly because of her advanced pregnancy. She said Krystal caught the last train home later that night and joined the family in the local pub. She said that Krystal was on edge and regularly checked her phone while at the hotel but the earlier telephone conversation wasn't mentioned again.

What is clear from these comments is that Peter Jenkinson was unequivocally involved with Krystal shortly before her disappearance and was allegedly owed money by her. On the basis of this information there can be little doubt that Krystal identified Peter Jenkinson as PJ. It was the moniker she alone applied to him as he was universally known by his friends simply as Pete. The fact that Jenkinson had allegedly spuriously told Krystal that he had a wife and kids is a further example of the inequitable nature of their relationship and his lack of genuine interest in her. The invention seemed designed purely to prevent exposure of his relationship with her.

Is it a possibility that Krystal's disappearance had absolutely nothing to do with the mystery caller? Could the answer to her disappearance on that night be attributable to some opportunistic assailant who happened across Krystal walking alone in an isolated area of the town? If this was the case, why didn't the mystery phone box caller ring Krystal back? More significantly, why was the phone box never used to ring Krystal's mobile again? The answer to that is that the caller knew exactly where she was and there was absolutely no reason to make such a call. Accordingly, the likelihood of an opportunistic attacker is rejected.

Peter Jenkinson failed to respond to my requests for an interview.

CHAPTER TWENTY-ONE
Missing Persons Squad

I have touched on my brief interactions with investigators attached to the missing persons squad previously. Most recently on a rebuke by Detective Brett Thexton following my attempts to speak to Craig 'Twiggy' Newton. Keen to keep a level of communication open between us, I sent Thexton transcripts of interviews I had conducted with David Toll, Ariee Toll, Kerryn Watson and 'Mandy' (not her real name), a former partner of Peter Jenkinson, who I will introduce in the following chapter.

These transcripts were forwarded on 16 November 2021. I considered they contained additional material relevant to the investigation. I have already illustrated the fabric of the intelligence obtained from David and Ariee Toll. Thexton responded via email on 10 February 2022, some three months later, advising me that the information I had forwarded '...was valuable and previously unknown.'

On 19 May 2022, Thexton and his supervising officer, the laid-back DetSgt Maurie Ryan, attended at my house by appointment. It was obvious from their demeanour that our relationship had been enriched.

Both were dedicated to the investigation and totally driven to solve the mystery of Krystal's disappearance. They told me they had interviewed Peter Jenkinson again a couple of weeks earlier. They touched on Jenkinson's previous admissions to having rung Krystal while she was in the Medihotel the week of her disappearance, Ryan telling me that Jenkinson was now, '...suffering amnesia and saying he didn't remember having rung her.'

Thexton said he believed that the details of my conversation with David Toll had created doubt in Toll's mind about Jenkinson's innocence telling me, 'He originally told investigators it was midnight when Jenkinson had left his place but he is now saying what he told you, and even broader, that he'd left his place between 10 and 11.00 pm. Your record of the conversation with him also had Jenkinson in his white ute, not the green car he told investigators at the time.'

I had previously raised Shannon Jones' name with Thexton on 15 February 2021 when he rang to chastise me over my call to Craig 'Twiggy' Newton. It was then that he had dismissed me, saying they had spoken to Shannon and obtained her statement. While sitting in my lounge room Thexton and Ryan told me they felt they had a strong circumstantial case against Peter Jenkinson, outlining that evidence, which was basically everything I have already covered.

I told them that they had more than circumstantial evidence in Shannon Jones. They looked at me blankly. I told them her evidence was direct primary evidence against Jenkinson over the death of Krystal. Unfortunately they were completely unaware of her information given my attempts to discuss this evidence fifteen months earlier.

Shannon Jones is the daughter of the previously scrutinised Steve Jones. I was put in touch with her by Sue McGillivray of Gunbower. Shannon told me that she was sixteen or seventeen and living with her father and younger brother Bradley in Gunbower at the time of Krystal's disappearance.

She said she was at Jenkinson's house with her father one evening, shortly before Krystal's disappearance, when she heard her father arguing with Peter Jenkinson about Krystal. She alleged Jenkinson was saying that Krystal would have to be killed and her father was yelling at him that she shouldn't.

She further alleged, 'Pete didn't want her to have the baby, but she wouldn't get rid of it. He had boars out the back of his property and I believe that's where he got rid of the bodies, but I have no evidence other than hearing him fight with my dad. Everyone's quick to blame dad and say it's all on him cause he's not here to defend himself. I know he was not the father, nor did he kill her.'

Shannon refused to elaborate on this or meet for an interview. She told me her family had told the police everything at the time.

Ryan and Thexton disclosed they had never heard this before. Thexton revealed they had spoken to Shannon and her former stepmother, Denise Jones, and this had never been divulged. They subsequently obtained a statement from Shannon (26 June 2022). She gave evidence at the inquest and elaborated on the brief synopsis she had provided to me. She told the court that she had told the police the same story as she had told me when her father was arrested at their Gunbower home (16 September 2009) in relation to Krystal's disappearance.

She said the police told her she was protecting her father and was too young. (She turned seventeen in November that year). She also said that she had heard Jenkinson and her father talking about Krystal on three or four occasions and knew that 'Pete and Krystal had been together and that she was pregnant and I'd heard it was his baby. Pete believed the child to be his and she wouldn't get rid of it. He either thought it was his or she told him it was his. Krystal wanted to keep the baby. Pete said during a conversation with dad that if she didn't get rid of the baby he would get rid of her. Dad said don't be fucking stupid, that's a mother and child, along those lines. And Jenkinson was like, "I'll just feed her to the pigs".'

Shannon also said that Pete used the words 'nuffy' and 'retarded' when he talked about Krystal.

Shannon further explained, 'Dad was yelling during this conversation about killing — giving her to the pigs. He shouted, "What the fuck are you talking about." They were raising their voices at one another. I also heard Pete telling dad that Krystal had rung him, think she wanted him at the hospital, he'd said no.'

Shannon's testimony was that this conversation took place at Jenkinson's place, saying that she was outside playing with Jenkinson's dog and moved close to the back door to listen when she overheard the men yelling. She claimed she heard, 'I will just chuck her to the pigs or the boar.' She said Jenkinson and her father were best mates and she had never heard them argue before; her father told her immediately afterwards that she could never go back to Jenkinson's place again, because '... they weren't friends anymore.'

She added that she didn't think the two men ever spoke again, '...until the day my father rang and said he was going to suicide and he'd said that he'd either spoken to him or saw him.'

Wayne Woltsche, in charge of the investigation between 2009 to 2018 was questioned about his knowledge of Shannon's evidence at the inquest. He said she had never been spoken to by police as 'I don't believe she was present or was with Mr Jones at that period of time and I believe that Jones was arrested by Bendigo detectives.'

There are a couple of points that need clarification. Woltsche acknowledged later in his evidence that he was aware of the note left with Sue McGillivray by Steve Jones, which was essentially a threat to Peter Jenkinson's life. He said he visited Jones and spoke to him on the back of it the day after Jones had written the memo (23 September 2009). Although the investigation wasn't being run by the Purana task force, as recorded by Steve Jones in his memo, it was being run by Woltsche.

Jones' notation, '...I told the head of the Purana task force that if they didn't get someone — preferably Sharon or Nick to my residence...' implied that Woltsche, and the homicide squad, were fully involved with Jones at this time, not the Bendigo CIU.

Indeed, Detectives Sharon Bell and Nick Densley were on Woltsche's crew and had been dealing with the Fraser family at the time. Undeniably, the homicide squad clearly had authority of the investigation by 16 September 2009, the day of Jones' arrest, as it had taken over the investigation from Bendigo CIU on 7 August 2009. The fact that Steve Jones specifically referred to 'Sharon' and 'Nick' on 23 September makes it evident that he met these two officers when arrested a few days earlier, the day of his first interaction with investigators in relation to Krystal's disappearance.

It really doesn't matter with whom Shannon Jones shared the incriminating evidence against Peter Jenkinson, but that there was no record of it is of great importance. Shannon gave evidence at the inquest that she wasn't sure to which police she provided the evidence of Jenkinson's felonious intent, '... as there were so many there that day.'

During my conversation with Ryan and Thexton at my house I advised them of the information supplied by Sue McGillivray. Again, they were completely unfamiliar with the material she had provided, the elements of which were identical to those she had presented to homicide officers in 2009.

Chapter Twenty-One Missing Persons Squad

They visited Sue that day and obtained a statement from her, the first statement she had been asked to make in relation to this matter. Her information clearly added further circumstantial evidence against Jenkinson.

My initial thoughts about the missing persons squad's investigation was that it had charged off after Craig 'Twiggy' Newton on the basis of the 'fresh' information received concerning him, without first referencing the homicide squad's investigation log. Critically, it had eliminated Newton in 2009 based on telephone logs and witnesses.

Wayne Woltsche's evidence in this regard at the inquest was, 'We checked his phone movement through towers and the times and locations were different to Krystal's and never lined up. I was comfortable that he wasn't involved and could not have been following extensive analysis of phone records and witnesses.'

Is it possible that this information did not appear in their log of the investigation? Was there also no reference to Sue McGillivray as there appears to have been no mention whatsoever of the salient information provided by Shannon Jones? One conclusion is that the missing persons squad investigators failed to address the homicide log. The other, more precarious inference is that the log lacked crucial details.

Given that it appears there was explicit evidence of Peter Jenkinson's intention to kill Krystal a short time before her disappearance, and a swathe of corroborative circumstantial evidence available in 2009, in all likelihood an arrest could have been made then, effectively shielding the Fraser family from many years of needless anxiety.

CHAPTER TWENTY-TWO
Peter Jenkinson's Relationships

Peter Jenkinson bought the Gunbower Island property he still lives in with his girlfriend of the time, a local woman who grew up on a nearby farm. I have spoken to this woman, whom I have decided not to name. She is bright, friendly and intelligent and leading her best life.

She told me that Jenkinson and she began a relationship when they were in their early twenties, enjoying similar interests of camping, fishing and hunting. She said he also hunted with pig dogs, catching pigs and occasionally taking them home to their property to breed and fatten up. She acknowledged that they also smoked a lot of marijuana and tried speed later in their relationship.

She said her interests changed over time and she became jaded with their lifestyle, particularly the drug taking. She added that Jenkinson's mother caused a little disharmony in their relationship also, '...because she didn't like me, considered me not good enough for their family.'

She said she ended her relationship with Jenkinson in 2003, about ten years after it had begun. She described

Jenkinson's demeanour during their time together as, '... normally very placid, the only time I saw him blow up was with his twin brother Shane. He was naturally a little angry after I broke up with him but there was never any violence towards me.'

It is not known when it began, but it has been confirmed that Jenkinson later started a relationship with an Asian woman who lived in Greensborough at the time. A subsequent long-term partner of Jenkinson told me that he fathered a child to this woman, a son who was born in 2008 or 2009. Denise Jones, Steve's former wife, referred to this woman as Nguyen and confirmed that Jenkinson and the woman had had a child together. Sources suggest that Jenkinson met this woman through Asian contacts involved in illegal cock fighting.

In December 2020, I met Jenkinson's long-term partner referred to above, who will be identified under the pseudonym of Mandy to ensure her anonymity. Again, Chantel helped make this meeting happen. Mandy was paranoid about her safety, expressing her fear of Peter Jenkinson. She said she met Jenkinson at the Southern 80 ski race, held at Echuca on the weekend of 12-14 February 2010. She was introduced to Jenkinson by a bikie known to both of them who told her that Jenkinson, '...had been accused of a horrible crime that he would never have committed.'

Mandy was living in a small rural community south of Echuca at the time, where she ran a twenty-five-horse stud farm. She also worked in animal husbandry in Bendigo. In describing Jenkinson, Mandy said, '...he was the nicest guy, but he had a lady in Melbourne at the time and they'd had a son together who was about two.'

Mandy said she went to Jenkinson's Gunbower home a couple of times soon after their first meeting and she observed a large pig in a pen at the property. Jenkinson allegedly warned her not to go near it as it would eat her. She said that he moved in with her more or less straight after they got together. She believed this was to avoid the scrutiny he had been experiencing in Gunbower over the Krystal Fraser investigation. She said Jenkinson also told her that he had been subjected to interviews by homicide squad officers and a search of his Gunbower property in relation to Krystal's disappearance shortly before they had met.

She said one night not long after Jenkinson had moved in with her, he received a phone call from his bikie mate, the one who had introduced them. Mandy said she overheard him tell Jenkinson, 'Hey Pete, fuck you're lucky you were at Mandy's place last night because fucking Steve Jones killed himself.' Jenkinson is alleged to have said, 'Oh really,' and the bikie had said, '...and he left a suicide note saying that he drove up to your place to kill you and was then gonna kill himself but that you weren't there so he just killed himself. I know it's true cause I saw the tyre marks.' Jenkinson is alleged to have simply responded with, 'Oh yeh.'

The precise details of the suicide note remain unknown to

me despite a request to the Victorian coroner's office for access to the file. The source of the bikie's information, however, is unknown and the alleged phraseology of the suicide note remains questionable.

Mark Ariens, the cop from Cohuna who responded to Jones' suicide, has no recollection of wording to this effect appearing in Jones' suicide note. It can also be argued that the suicide note would have been seized by police at the earliest opportunity, meaning it should not have been available to others to view.

Mandy said Jenkinson had gone shooting the previous night and he had gone out alone; she couldn't remember him ever going shooting alone other than on this occasion. She said she thought his reaction to the news of Jones' suicide was puzzling and was surprised when he hadn't mentioned that he'd been out shooting during the call to his mate.

She said she hadn't thought much of this at the time but began thinking more about it when she learned years later that Steve Jones was shot in the stomach, which she felt was very unusual. Despite her feelings, there is nothing to support an inference or suspicion that Jenkinson, or anyone else, was in any way involved with Jones' death or that the examining coroner's finding of suicide was inaccurate.

Mandy said that Jenkinson never discussed Jones' possible involvement in Krystal's disappearance. She said he led her to believe that the two men had been good friends, but that Jones had fallen out with him because Jenkinson had attracted the attention of police over the investigation into Krystal's disappearance, impacting on Jones' drug dealing. This is the premise she said Jenkinson presented to her.

Mandy said she learned the extent of Jenkinson's previous relationship with the Asian woman when he told her that he needed to travel to Melbourne to see his son. She said she amiably accepted this and at first he would travel down and back to visit him on the same day.

She said she suggested to Jenkinson that she should accompany him and get to know his son. Mandy said he told her that the boy's mother wouldn't like her and that it wasn't his place to invite strangers to her house. She said she then proposed that his son could stay at her place, and Jenkinson told her that the boy's mother wouldn't agree to this. Mandy said she couldn't understand why she was excluded from that part of her partner's life.

Not long after Jenkinson had started making the regular trips to visit his son in Melbourne Mandy said he began staying the night at his former partner's home. Mandy said that this wasn't prearranged with her and a pattern began to emerge with Jenkinson turning his phone off when this occurred. She said he explained to her that he was sleeping on the couch when he stayed over but was unable to provide a satisfactory excuse for turning his phone off, insisting that there was nothing going on with the woman.

Mandy said she felt that Jenkinson had lost interest in her when, after breaking her leg, Jenkinson went off with his bikie friend, '...leaving me like a dog, with a pile of wood to keep the fire going. I felt like a dog, a normal person would have stayed and cared for me.' Around this time she discovered from Jenkinson's sister that they were doing up his home in Gunbower. She said when she asked Jenkinson about this he told her his son was coming to stay for the weekend. She couldn't understand why he wouldn't bring the child to her house.

Shortly after this Mandy said she had a cataract removed and when Jenkinson picked her up from the hospital afterwards he left his wallet in her car. She said she was aware that he was planning to visit his son that weekend and would need his wallet. She said she rang him to tell him about it and while on the phone to him opened the wallet and found a condom inside. She said she challenged him angrily over the find and he told her that the condom had been there for years. She said it hadn't, and told him so.

Mandy said this behaviour and her suspicions about his actual relationship with his former partner caused her to have a breakdown, and they broke up at this point. She added that they'd been in the relationship for about three years at this stage and she had never met Jenkinson's parents.

* * *

Mandy said she sold her horse stud and moved to another northern Victorian country town following the split in 2013 before moving to Tasmania for twelve months. She said that despite their breakup, Jenkinson and she remained in contact and he visited her regularly before she moved to Tasmania. She said following her return to Victoria he eventually convinced her to move in with him at his Gunbower property in 2016 and told her the Asian woman had become a resident of Thailand and no longer represented a threat to their relationship.

Mandy said she learned that Jenkinson had been with another woman from northeast Victoria in her absence but Jenkinson convinced her that this relationship had ended. She said she discovered that the relationship wasn't over when the other woman began ringing Jenkinson. Mandy alleged that he visited this other woman and after his return she overheard him speaking to her on the phone, saying she rang the number back after the call had ended and asked the woman what was going on.

She said this woman abused her, and the woman's daughter had rung Jenkinson on his mobile in the meantime. Mandy alleged that Jenkinson rushed up to her and said, 'You're nothing to me you fucking cunt.' Mandy said this, 'Ripped my heart out, especially as the woman and her daughter were still listening as Pete was still on the phone to them.' She said she and Jenkinson had an argument following this and he smashed her mobile. She claimed that during the argument he grabbed her by the hair, threw her to the ground and stood on her head.

Mandy said she went to the police in Echuca and reported

the incident but chose not to mention Jenkinson's name, stating that she was only seeking advice about where she stood and the fact that he had guns in the house. She said that when she returned to the house she made the mistake of telling Jenkinson that if he was violent towards her again he would lose his guns. She alleged he had figured that she'd been to the police and as a result went into a rage and told her to pack her belongings and get out. She said that he then, 'Ran around killing all the chooks, he killed about thirty by breaking their necks, I was running along behind him crying stop, please stop. He just went mad killing all these animals.'

Mandy alleged that Jenkinson then had police attend and had her removed from the property, without explanation. She said that this was in June or July 2018. It is not known what authority police used to evict her. She said that she told these police officers about Jenkinson's destruction of the fowls and alleges she was told that he was able to deal with his own property as he saw fit. The killing, as described, sounds very much like a breach of the Protection of Animals Act.

Following their split, Mandy said that with assistance of Anglicare she moved to central Victoria and stayed there with friends. She said Jenkinson soon contacted her again and began visiting, taking her gold detecting occasionally. After he convinced her that his relationship with the other woman was over she moved back in with him in late 2018.

Mandy said she had been receiving counselling following the initial breakdown of her relationship with Jenkinson. Her counsellor had rung her about nine months into this most recent union with Jenkinson and she had told her that this period had been the happiest of her life and that she couldn't imagine life without Jenkinson. But then her life was turned upside down again when she discovered Jenkinson was seeing a New Zealand backpacker who was working for his employer in a casual seasonal role.

Mandy said she found an image online of Jenkinson holding the New Zealand woman's hand. She said she asked him about the woman and he told her that there was nothing in it, claiming he was responsible for entertaining the backpackers for his employer. According to Mandy, Jenkinson kept going out every night and not coming home and was allegedly locking his phone and internet.

During this period, Mandy said a friend of hers gave her a copy of the *Herald Sun* with a front page reading, 'Massive reward to solve tragic cold case.' The article related to a million-dollar reward for information in relation to Krystal's disappearance.

I spoke to the person who provided her with the *Herald Sun* in January 2021. He confirmed this, telling me that he was going through a separation at that point and Mandy was ringing constantly, '...checking up on me.' A local dairy farmer, he was aware that Jenkinson had been a suspect in the case and thought it was in Mandy's interests to see the article. The newspaper was dated Wednesday 17 July 2019.

Mandy said she took the paper home and pointed out the

front page and the following article to Jenkinson saying, 'You better pull your head in Pete; people are going to be watching you. He glared at me and I said jokingly we could make a million dollars by saying Steve Jones did it and he continued to glare at me and said, "What do you mean?" I repeated what I'd said and he glared even more.'

She said she then confronted him about the other woman, '...in a mature manner, as I didn't want to antagonise him, I said to him, where is this going to end Pete? She is from New Zealand.'

Mandy said that Jenkinson flung the newspaper and everything else that was on the kitchen bench on to the floor and said, 'This is how your life's going to be, you fucking cunt. You've outdone your welcome.' Mandy continued, 'He was totally someone I didn't know, the look in his eyes. I was too scared to move.' She further alleged that he said, 'Don't you even light a cigarette, you cunt, don't you fuck with me, you cunt.' Mandy said she couldn't believe how what she'd said could have triggered such a response. Was his overreaction a consequence of the reference to the New Zealand backpacker or the implications posed by the newspaper article he was shown?

Mandy said Jenkinson went out following this and didn't come home again that night but when he returned the following evening he tried to get her phone from her. She alleged that he had smashed four or five of her phones over the years, 'If he didn't like what I'd written, or there were pictures of me with black eyes.'

Chapter Twenty-Two Peter Jenkinson's Relationships

Asked to elaborate on this she said that he had blackened an eye once when he hit her. She added that Jenkinson had also once twisted her back causing her to consult a chiropractor whom she asked to report the issue to police. She said all the incidents of violence arose when she questioned him about other women. According to her, she never challenged him, simply asked questions.

On this, what was to be the final occasion, she said she tried to prevent Jenkinson from getting her phone, '...as I had been making comments to my sister on Facebook about his behaviour the previous day.' She said Jenkinson got her phone off her by punching her in the ribs with a powerful uppercut, which caused immediate severe pain. 'He then took my phone outside and began going through it before smashing it against a steel post and then destroying it by stamping his foot on it on the ground.'

She said he then drove off in a rage, returning later without saying a word and then leaving again. She added, 'I have never felt such fear as when he went off that night, the look in his eyes and all I thought of was Krystal Fraser. I remember him saying one night, you think I did it, too, when we were talking about Krystal and I told him he was scaring me.'

Mandy said she had a computer hidden in her room that Jenkinson was unaware of and used it to contact her sister overseas during the night. I viewed a Facebook message on Mandy's account sent to her sister at 4.37 am on 19 July 2019, which reads, 'He went mental, smashed my phone and

I think I have broken ribs.' This message confirms the timing of the incident and verifies Mandy's accusations. Mandy said she consulted a doctor later that morning and told him the circumstances of the assault. She said the doctor advised her that he thought her ribs were bruised and not broken.

Mandy wanted to run but was scared of what Jenkinson might do to her animals so returned to his property with a plan to get the animals out first. Jenkinson's violence towards her, as described, occurred after he became aware of the million-dollar reward and the news that, 'Fresh information from the public earlier this year refocused the investigation on a man interviewed by police early in the case.' (*Herald Sun*, 17/7/2019).

Mandy accepted that her relationship with Jenkinson was over and was in the process of organising the removal of her animals, which included two horses. She said, '...by this stage Pete just came and went, didn't talk to me, was a totally different person, had a blank look in his eyes.' She said the one night he did stay at the property, and was sleeping on the couch, she was unable to sleep because of the pain in her ribs and phoned an on-call doctor around four in the morning. She said Jenkinson said to her, 'What are you doing on the phone this time of night, you fucking cunt, I'm trying to sleep?' She said, 'He just broke me.'

She said she drove herself to the Echuca Hospital and staff organised for Anglicare to put her in a motel room so that she could get some sleep. She said she rang Jenkinson to advise him what had been arranged for her and she alleged he said, 'Well if you do that don't expect to see your animals when you get back.'

Mandy said that after she had removed all her animals off Jenkinson's property and had shifted in with friends, she went to the Shepparton police station to report his assault on her. She wanted Jenkinson charged over this most recent assault but was scared that if she proceeded with charges the police would seize his guns and he would come after her animals. She said she was forced to withdraw her complaint when the police recorded her current (safe haven) address on the intervention order served on Jenkinson. She said that as a result, her friends providing refuge for her literally threw her out on the street through fear.

Mandy said that during the entire time she was with Jenkinson, Krystal Fraser was hardly ever mentioned. She said that Jenkinson did tell her early in their relationship that he had been in a sexual relationship with Krystal, '...but had stopped seeing her that way well before her pregnancy.'

Not long before their relationship ended, according to Mandy, she was at home and saw what she believed were police divers searching the channel that runs along the western boundary of Jenkinson's property. She said she rang Jenkinson and told him of her observations, and he told her that they wouldn't have been police, they would have been scientists searching for turtles. Mandy added that at the same time as the divers were in the channel there was a drone going over the property. She said she advised Jenkinson of this also and was told it would have just been State Rivers checking the irrigation channels.

Shortly before the media conference on 17 July 2019, Karen Fraser said Detective Damon Abby of the missing persons squad rang her and advised her that he, along with a number of police divers, were searching several waterways in the Gunbower area that day. He told her he was letting her know in case the media got hold of the story and began ringing her. Karen said she was never informed of the result of these searches.

Mandy said that on one occasion she and Jenkinson were discussing police interviews and he is alleged to have told her that he could easily outlie a lie detector, '…it was simply a matter of believing your own lies.'

CHAPTER TWENTY-THREE

McGillivray Abattoirs

The McGillivray name is well known in the Gunbower district. It is synonymous with sporting achievements throughout the region and beyond. The name is currently associated with the popular local gastropub, a café, service station, butchery, hairdressing salon, electrical services and farming. And, for sixty years, McGillivray Abattoirs. The abattoirs closed in 2017 when in the hands of Gary McGillivray, known as Jack, who ran the business with his mother, Gwen, following the death of his father ten years earlier.

Jack McGillivray is now retired, a carer for his chronically ill wife. Contrary to the opinions of many, he was open to a conversation. McGillivray is well known in the district for his staunch advocacy for the conservation of the Gunbower national park and its array of magnificent waterways. He has wild hair and a ruthless aspect, still muscular but much older looking than his sixty years.

He told me he was kicked out of school and unable to read and write at fourteen, but in adulthood achieved a degree in microbiology to help him write manuals for the operation of his business and stay ahead of government compliance. While he acknowledged his business folded because it was losing money, unable to compete with supermarket chains, he feels it was adversely affected by constant rumours linking the abattoirs to Krystal's disappearance. The business was even named explicitly in an *Age* article of 23 June 2012, with the following, 'Already the district was rife with rumours about the abattoirs, including McGillivray's, and the sick talk went that Krystal's body had been disposed of, minced and fed to pigs.'

When I asked him about these rumours he said, 'Apparently I ran her through a mincer, but I don't have a mincer. It's malicious slander.'

I advised him that a person of interest in the case had allegedly made statements to the effect that Krystal's body had been disposed of into a truck at an abattoir after she was put through a mincer there. He responded with, 'The business was a Monday to Friday job; the girl went missing on a Saturday night. Whenever we planned to do a kill we would advise Pridham's, who operated the offal truck to make a collection. If we weren't doing a kill we wouldn't ring them. We would throw the guts of all the slaughtered animals into a bulk bin which would get loaded on to the gut truck, as we called it, by the driver. On weekends the offal bins were always empty; if someone threw something into one of the bins I would have noticed it. There were no lights at the abattoir, it was a daytime operation. I know when someone comes down my driveway, and if some cunt's over there (the abattoirs), I'll front them straight away. I might be a cold-hearted cunt but I don't believe anyone has the right to kill another person.'

McGillivray lives in an impressive solid red brick property he built himself on the banks of the Gunbower Creek on Gunbower Island. His house is about seventy metres from the former abattoir. Following a series of questions about the operation of the abattoir, McGillivray said, 'Before the guts truck, when we started here, we used to mince everything up, throw it in a copper and boil it up to feed the pigs. Then we'd take all the bones out and crush them up with a bone cruncher and put it on our property as fertiliser. When the government said we couldn't do that anymore we got a big Kato (excavator) in and dug big holes and filled it up with all the offal. When the government stopped us doing that, we got Pridham's. There is shit buried everywhere. If you started digging, well fuck man, it would be an archaeological nightmare.'

Quizzed about the existence of a mincer given that he had only just said that he didn't have one, he said, 'That's years ago. I have a big one over there I could run you through it, but I bought it as an antique. I've never had it going in my entire life. It's got a huge electric motor on it and you'd never get it going without changing the transformer. The transformer in the abs is not big enough.'

Asked why he thought the suspicions regarding him and his business in relation to Krystal had endured, he said, 'The fuckin' cops keep coming back and grilling me, asking me the same stupid questions, they pass the case on to a new couple and they come out and rehash it. They ask the same questions and I tell them the same fuckin' things — Yeh I've got a mincer but the fuckin' thing doesn't work and that it would be highly unlikely for anyone to have put her in a bin. Everyone gets to hear about their visits and the suspicion never fades away.'

When I raised the topic of Steve Jones' association with the abattoirs and suggestions that he may have been involved in Krystal's disappearance, he offered, 'He was a fucking nut case and if you do your mathematics, it works out to be, you know what I mean. If you analyse and profile everything it just makes sense to me that that is who done it. I've got nothing concrete, it's just supposition, my point of view, he's the guy that shot himself and he was bipolar. The criteria fits if you profile him and analyse things. Because you can't live with that, some people can, others can't live with it. Empathy is what it is called, and guilt, you can only hide from that for so long, then all of a sudden...'

McGillivray confirmed that at the time of Krystal's disappearance Steve Jones was living in rented premises on a farm property less than a kilometre from the Gunbower Abattoirs.

McGillivray acknowledged that he knew Krystal as she used to work in one of the butcher shops he supplied (Pyramid Hill). He had heard that she was buying ice (crystal methamphetamine) from a dealer in Bendigo, adding that he had never done any business with her. While he didn't elaborate on the nature of this 'business,' he divulged that he had done business with the Morans, Tony Mokbel and Carl Williams. He added, 'People know them, but smart crooks, people don't know about, and don't get caught. That was my lifestyle, but I'm retired now.'

When probed about the legitimacy of his 'retirement,' McGillivray, for a man who's story is rooted in the tougher realities of the underworld, showed a completely contradictory side to his character, offering, 'My son hung himself when he was twenty-three and it devastated me, and I had to change my life. I had shown my children a lifestyle that was not normal. And it cost me my son to realise that. He was trying to follow in my footsteps, we didn't live a normal life, it was full of drugs and violence and lots of shit. I didn't realise, I was busy leading and I wasn't looking back, and I should have. And now I do counselling for people whose kids have committed suicide. My son went and hung himself after I gave him a beating when he came to the house with a gun on Christmas Day and threatened the family. It was my fault; my wife blames me and I accept it. It's reality. That's why I hide in drugs and drink all the time — living with it. Can't get away from guilt, guilt, guilt.'

McGillivray's son had been hospitalised a number of times before his death in relation to a mental health disorder. His death preceded Krystal's disappearance.

While it is true that apparatus used to slaughter and butcher stock was available at the abattoirs, and despite the rumours implicating McGillivray in the disappearance of Krystal, there is simply no evidence that he was involved. It also appears implausible that someone else, without his knowledge and consent, would have attended at the abs and used the equipment there to assist in the mutilation of Krystal's body.

While it is reasonable to assume that Steve Jones would have known how to operate the abattoir's equipment and was familiar with the operation of the plant he would not have been able to use the complex without McGillivray's consent or knowledge. Consideration should also be given to the seemingly legitimate attempts Jones undertook to uncover evidence against the person or persons responsible for Krystal's disappearance. He never spoke of any suspicions about the abs or McGillivray and spent time searching a farm property near Pyramid Hill looking for Krystal's body. Of course, if he was the killer and he did use the abs, it would be in his interests to direct the investigation away from there.

Why would McGillivray put himself and his business interests, both legitimate and nefarious, if any, at risk, by allowing someone else to dispose of a body there? Police investigators involved in Krystal's disappearance have never raised the existence of a link between McGillivray and Krystal. Indeed, Wayne Woltsche of the homicide squad was quoted in the *Age* (23 June 2012), 'I've seen no evidence to support the abs side of things.'

Furthermore, if Krystal's killer was driven by a strong personal motive, such as avoiding maintenance costs, or preventing the revelation of an intimate personal relationship with a woman with an intellectual disability, why recruit another or others into the criminality, potentially increasing the risk of exposure?

Jack McGillivray described himself as a smart guy. Smart guys don't risk exposure by getting involved in someone else's personal affairs.

CHAPTER TWENTY-FOUR

Where Is Krystal?

Dr Kim Rossmo, a geographic profiling expert and chair of the school of Criminal Justice and Criminology at Texas State University, advocates that most crimes occur close to the offender's home, often within a kilometre. His research has shown that as offenders move further away from their home the probability that they will offend decreases. He further contends that body dump sites tend to be further from the killer's residence[17]. A forensic examination of Krystal's flat failed to establish a crime scene there, suggesting that Krystal was murdered elsewhere. Notwithstanding the fact that the site was tainted if Krystal had been murdered there, some scientific evidence should have been discovered.

Does the information derived from the telco towers help provide a reliable theory in relation to the location of her death and the site of her burial? Assuming that the killer had to travel from Leitchville, following the 11.59 pm call from the phone box to Krystal in Pyramid Hill, it would have taken about seventeen minutes, driving at the speed limit, before this person arrived at Krystal's location in Pyramid

Hill. Assuming, of course, that the caller left immediately after the call.

Telco records show that Krystal's phone was connected to the Pyramid Hill tower when she received this last call from the Leitchville phone box at 11.59 pm. Her phone was still 'pinging' off the Pyramid Hill tower eighteen minutes later, at 0.17.09 am, when her mobile was used to access data.

Her phone was similarly used at 1.45 am. On this occasion it was connected to the Patho tower. And at 2.49 am the phone was used for the last time and switched off; at that time, it was connected to the Leitchville tower.

Media coverage of these details throughout the years have all suggested that Krystal moved from one tower to another at these times. According to Telstra expert Tim Miller, this is false.

While it is true that her phone moved between 00.17 and 2.49 am, the timing of its progress from one location to another is unknown. As a mobile phone will only need to engage with a phone tower when in use, the last known tower would show on records until the phone is used within the reception area of a new tower. The phone has to be either getting or giving data to Telstra to be picked up by a tower. Consequently, all that can be said in relation to the phone's movement, irrespective of Krystal's movements, as she may have not remained with her phone; is that her phone was connected to the Pyramid Hill tower at 17 minutes past midnight, the Patho tower at 1.45 am and the Leitchville tower at 2.49 am.

While the timing of the phone's movement between these three locations cannot be accurately determined, the fact that it has moved between these locations is discernible. It is also evident that Krystal, or her mobile at least, did not venture outside a relatively small geographical area. If so, it would have been picked up by additional phone towers within the neighbouring shires of Loddon, Gannawarra and Campaspe.

A speculative explanation for Krystal's journey, assuming she was picked up in Pyramid Hill, is that the killer or killers would have avoided the main thoroughfare of the Leitchville-Pyramid Hill Road, taking one of two unsealed roadways that link Pyramid Hill and Gunbower.

It is appropriate to infer that the vehicle conveying Krystal travelled in this easterly direction after leaving Pyramid Hill as Krystal's phone moved from the Pyramid Hill tower to the Patho tower, which covered Gunbower at the time, and finally the Leitchville tower. If the initial journey had been from Pyramid Hill to Leitchville, Krystal's phone would have been picked up by the Leitchville tower at 1.45 am rather than the Patho tower. This clearly suggests that her journey (or that of her phone) was due east in the Gunbower/Patho direction and not northeast to Leitchville. It should be established that Patho is a rural agricultural area, its infrastructure consisting of nothing more than a landfill site and a cemetery. There are no other community structures.

The first of these two alternate routes is via the Pyramid-Echuca Road, which runs off the 'major' Leitchville-Pyramid

Hill Road to the east a few kilometres north of Pyramid Hill, on the Leitchville side of town. This backroad runs through an isolated rural area with not one visible dwelling. As it has been established that Krystal's phone was receiving its signal from the Patho tower at 1.45 am, and a little over an hour later, when it was turned off, the Leitchville tower, it is possible that she was murdered somewhere along this back road. The fact that Krystal's phone was being used at 1.45-1.46 am to access data supports the theory that the killer or killers did this after her death, conceivably in an attempt to learn if she had communicated the details of her meeting with the killer on social media or via a text message.

The time between the 1.45-1.46 am operation of Krystal's phone within the scope of the Patho tower and the 2.49 am use while connected to the Leitchville tower may have been used to dispose of Krystal's body.

The Pyramid-Echuca Road intersects with the Murray Valley Highway five kilometres south of Gunbower. Almost immediately after exiting on to the Murray Valley Highway towards Gunbower a right turn on to Gibbon Road leads to Gunbower Island and numerous permanent water bodies. This route from Pyramid Hill to Gunbower, on inferior unsealed roads, avoids all major thoroughfares and towns.

The timing of the meeting with Krystal may have been influenced by the killer knowing that local cops generally knocked off at midnight on Saturdays. If Krystal's death was premeditated, the killer or killers could not have afforded to risk being intercepted or detected with Krystal in their vehicle. The quickest and conventional journey from Pyramid Hill to Gunbower would involve travel on the Leitchville-Pyramid Hill Road to Leitchville and then on the Murray Valley Highway to Gunbower.

The alternative backroads route between Pyramid Hill and Gunbower is via another unsealed rural road known as Normans Bridge Road. There would have been a greater risk of detection using this road as it runs off the main Leitchville-Pyramid Road some 13 kilometres north of Pyramid Hill. However, it is another route that is generally only used by rural property holders. There are a number of houses on this carriageway though, unlike the isolated Pyramid-Echuca Road.

A brief explanation of how a mobile phone 'finds' a phone tower or base station, as they are also known, is that it will connect to the nearest or least congested one nearby. Rural towers generally have a radius of five to thirty-two kilometres but their coverage will be limited by environmental obstructions such as trees, hills and large buildings between a phone and a tower[18]. The towers are strategically spaced to overlap and reception strength will normally be greatest within the range of the closest tower but Tim Miller warns that signal strength can also be affected by the number of phones 'connected' to a tower at any given time.

Following are the locations of the three telco towers providing reception to Krystal's mobile phone that night,

and the distances the towers were from neighbouring communities (the most direct path):
- Pyramid Hill - Leitchville 24 - Gunbower 26 - Patho 32
- Leitchville - Gunbower 9 - Patho 19 - Pyramid Hill 24
- Patho - Gunbower 10 - Leitchville 19 - Pyramid Hill 32

From this information it is reasonable to suggest that the telco signal in Gunbower could have been provided by either the Leitchville or Patho tower as it lies almost in the centre of the two locations. Gunbower is ten kilometres west of the Patho tower and nine kilometres east of the Leitchville tower.

When the locations of the towers and the distances between each are taken into consideration, the notion that the killer would have taken the Pyramid-Echuca Road after leaving Pyramid Hill is probable.

While only the killer knows precisely what occurred, it is reasonable to accept that Krystal's mobile signal would have been provided by the Leitchville tower and not the Patho tower, if her journey after leaving Pyramid Hill was towards Leitchville.

With the Leitchville tower only twenty-four kilometres from Pyramid Hill and the Patho tower some thirty-two kilometres away clearly, at 1.45 am, Krystal's phone must have been closer to Patho than Leitchville for it to have been connected to the Patho tower.

On the basis of this analysis and information regarding the

locations of Krystal's mobile at various times it is reasonable to assume she was transported along the Pyramid-Echuca Road after leaving Pyramid Hill sometime after 00.17 am on 21 June 2009.

Despite having a Gunbower address, Peter Jenkinson's property on Gunbower Island is located approximately six kilometres from the Leitchville tower and almost double that distance from the Patho tower. It is more likely that when at home his mobile would have been receiving reception from the Leitchville tower, which is the tower Krystal's mobile was connected to when last used to access data at 2.49 am on 21 June 2009 before being turned off for good.

Examination of the mud map may help show how Krystal's mobile phone signal offers an approximation of her possible locations after leaving Pyramid Hill that night, bearing in mind that a tower's signal strength is strongest the closer a mobile phone is to the tower.

* * *

The chatter linking the Gunbower Abattoirs to Krystal's dismemberment is overshadowed by rumours concerning the use of pigs in the destruction of Krystal's body. Indeed, the McGillivray abattoir was killing four hundred pigs a week at the time of its closure.

As the business engaged in the buying, fattening, killing

and ultimate sale of the product, it is reasonable to assume that there was always a number of pigs on the property. As a pig can consume three to five per cent of its body weight a day, about a kilogram for a mature animal, clearly a human body could have been consumed rapidly. However, pigs can't chew larger bones, instead breaking them up over time to make them manageable. Nor can pigs digest human teeth or hair, which they will leave behind[19]. The larger bones, hair and teeth plainly present a problem for anyone using pigs for this purpose, thus increasing the risk of discovery. Unless, that is, a mincer has first been used on the body. Even though a wild boar, the type kept by Peter Jenkinson, can grow to an enormous size, and will readily attack and eat humans given an opportunity, it would be impossible for a single animal to readily consume a body.

Given the vastness of the waterways in and around Gunbower, including the Murray River and Kow Swamp, the most credible explanation for the location of Krystal's final resting place is in the water. While decomposition is generally slower in water than on land, a body in the water may well be destroyed more quickly by freshwater crustaceans such as crayfish, yabbies and shrimp[20].

Dumping a corpse in a body of water involves little preparation. It is simply a matter of selecting a site, having some kind of weight to prevent the body floating during decomposition and something to attach the weight to the body. This would work whether the murder was premeditated or spontaneous if a suitable body of water existed nearby. Local anglers and hunters would have an excellent knowledge of the region's waterways and an appreciation of those that maintain water during extended drought.

Several kilometres off the Normans Bridge Road, which becomes the Gunbower-Pyramid Road after crossing Mt Hope Creek, abuts the lake known as Kow Swamp which covers twenty-four square kilometres adjacent to Leitchville and Gunbower. A three-kilometre stretch of this roadway, running in a north-south direction alongside the lake, ends when the road takes a ninety degree right turn at Dehne Road. The property on the southeast corner of the intersection belonged to David Toll, the former lawyer who provided the alibi for Peter Jenkinson. This road enters the township of Gunbower opposite the pub and the road to Gunbower Island.

Gibbon Road, referenced in the discussion about the potential route taken by Krystal's killer and which runs off the Murray Valley Highway just north of the intersection with Pyramid-Echuca Road, borders a number of watercourses. This dirt road, starting five kilometres south of Gunbower, becomes Richards Road and ultimately leads to Gunbower Island and the Murray River beyond. After leaving the highway and en route to Gunbower the road crosses Longmore Lagoon, also running alongside it, Phyland Lagoon and Gunbower Creek. All are potential sites to immerse a body.

CHAPTER TWENTY-FIVE

Coronial Inquest

The inquest into Krystal's disappearance was held over seven sitting days from 11 to 20 July 2022. Evidence was received from twenty-two witnesses. It was conducted by Coroner Katherine Lorenz and there were four lawyers representing various parties. Counsel assisting the coroner was Ms Fiona Batten. Mr Andrew Imrie represented the Chief Commissioner of Police, Mr Huw Roberts acted for Chantel Fraser and Ms Emma Strugnell appeared on behalf of Peter Jenkinson.

The Coroner's Court has jurisdiction to investigate deaths that appear to be unexpected, unnatural or violent, or to have resulted directly or indirectly from an accident or injury. Under the Coroner's Act, death is defined to include a suspected death. The existence of a body is not necessary. The coroner has a number of responsibilities pursuant to the Coroner's Act; she must make a finding on whether Krystal is deceased and, if so, the cause and circumstances of her death. And while the coroner is prevented under the Act from proclaiming any persons guilty of an offence, she can identify a person she believes may have caused Krystal's death.

The coroner handed down her findings on 13 October 2022.

I had completed writing up the results of my inquiries in relation to Krystal's disappearance before the inquest and have edited various segments throughout as a result of those proceedings.

Unknown to me, and the Fraser family, was a statement made previously by Alex Kristic in relation to the case in 2009. Alex is a former detective senior sergeant who had resigned before Krystal's disappearance to start his own business. His evidence provides further circumstantial evidence in the matter.

A keen hunter, Kristic had occasionally hunted deer with Peter Jenkinson and Steve Jones over a number of years before 2009. He had known Jones for a longer period in his working capacity as a detective when Jones had been a prison warder in the Latrobe Valley.

He said that Peter Jenkinson had been to his house in Melbourne once or twice previously when he turned up unexpectedly in August 2009. Kristic said they had a casual conversation about hunting and his dogs and then Jenkinson said, '...had a visit from the coppers about that sheila that went missing.' Kristic said he was unaware of what Jenkinson was talking about and questioned him about it, saying that Jenkinson replied, 'A sheila from up our way.'

Kristic was ignorant of Krystal's disappearance at the time and said he asked Jenkinson if he had been 'porking' the girl, figuring that Jenkinson may have had some relationship with her based on the way he was talking. Kristic alleged that Jenkinson said, 'No way, she's a bloody drug-fucked nuffy.'

Kristic also stated that Jenkinson asked, 'What do coppers normally do when they investigate that sort of thing?' He added that Jenkinson had never before asked about police procedures.

Kristic said shortly after this he received a phone call from Steve Jones in which Jones had said, 'The feds are up here. They're staying in Cohuna and they're talking to witnesses.' Kristic said he asked Jones what he was talking about and Jones replied, 'You know that sheila that went missing.' Kristic said he had seen something in relation to Krystal Fraser's disappearance around this time and had some knowledge of the case. He said Jones said to him, 'She'd been telling everyone that she was pregnant to Peter and that she was carrying his kid.' Kristic said he told Jones that the feds did not normally do missing persons enquiries and Jones was '…adamant that it was the feds and said, "they are after Peter, and he is paranoid".' Kristic said that Jones asked him to find out what was going on in the investigation. Kristic said given the fact that Jenkinson and Jones had made similar enquiries and there was media coverage of the incident they were discussing, he was suspicious. As a result, he provided investigators with his information.

* * *

While there were reports of a sighting outside the Bendigo post office and a retail store in the city, both dismissed as erroneous, there has never been a confirmed sighting of Krystal since 20 June 2009. Her failure to access her bank account (into which the public trustee has continued to deposit funds), her not seeking healthcare, despite the imminent birth of her child, and zero contact with her family all lead to one explanation: Krystal is dead.

Despite this universal assessment, contention arose over a Telstra record which appeared to show two calls from Krystal's mobile at 2.01 pm and 2.03 pm on 24 June 2009.

These were of particular interest to Peter Jenkinson's counsel as the police case throughout the inquiry suggested that Krystal was killed following the 11.59 pm call from the Leitchville phone box on 20 June 2009. Evidence that Krystal used her phone four days later clearly suggested that she was alive as the calls were to Krystal's brother, Aaron.

Following some initial confusion, Tim Miller of Telstra was able to provide a conclusive explanation for this contradiction. His testimony was that the activity on Krystal's phone appearing to have occurred on 24 June was generated on 20 June 2009. He said these were not calls but MMS messages. He explained that when a message is sent, it is sent to Telstra, not to the intended recipient, and that Telstra will then forward it to the planned receiver. It is a two-stage process. If the sender did not have credit, as he insisted was the case here, then Telstra would 'hang on' to the message until the phone was in credit. He added that as the number of messages being sent was so large Telstra would only 'hang on' to them for so long and then delete them. He insisted that the 2.01 pm and 2.03 pm notations were simply a record of when the system had deleted the messages. They were never sent to Aaron's phone as Krystal's phone continued to have no credit.

Miller confirmed there was absolutely no connection between Krystal's phone and Telstra after 2.49 am on 21 June 2009 when the phone was turned off. The last outgoing call on Krystal's phone occurred at 8.07 pm on 20 June 2009, to 125888, a Telstra number used to determine how much credit you have on your phone. The 00.17 am and 1.45 am communications related to the transfer of data only and were not phone calls.

* * *

Further evidence was provided by Tim Miller from his examination of relevant call history, in relation to an anomaly he discovered.

Although it was established that Krystal was using two mobile phones at the time of her disappearance, the number of the phone used most frequently ended in 924. During his record of interview with police Jenkinson was asked Krystal's mobile number and recited it with the last three digits rearranged — 942, instead of 924.

Records showed that Jenkinson had similarly rearranged the last three numbers twice in an identical fashion when he attempted to ring Krystal's mobile on 21 May 2008, as shown in the following table:

Date	Time	No called
21/05/2008	13.31.09	04......942
21/05/2008	13.31.10	04......942
21/05/2008	13.32.49	04......924

The caller from the Leitchville phone box also dialled the identical <u>wrong</u> sequence of numbers twice before ringing Krystal's number almost twelve months later, as follows:

Date	Time	No called
15/05/2009	21.09.39	04......942
15/05/2009	21.10.26	04......942
15/05/2009	21.11.00	04......924

The time of the 15 May 2009 call approximated to the time of other calls to Krystal's mobile from the Leitchville phone box between 14 May and 20 June 2009:

Date	Time	Duration (seconds)
14/05/2009	21.35.46	0
14/05/2009	21.36.40	0
14/05/2009	21.38.02	66

Date	Time	Duration (seconds)
15/05/2009	21.11.00	158
17/05/2009	21.19.16	100
21/05/2009	19.22.16	96
22/05/2009	19.55.38	159
22/05/2009	21.51.37	140
01/06/2009	19.16.36	70
06/06/2009	17.54.11	5
06/06/2009	17.54.50	5
06/06/2009	17.55.26	5
06/06/2009	17.56.01	5
09/06/2009	21.10.59	0
16/06/2009	19.45.19	182
19/06/2009	20.53.20	139
20/06/2009	17.42.23	80
20/06/2009	23.59.21	40

* * *

Debate over the protection of the crime scene continued at the hearing.

Wayne Woltsche said Victoria Police crime scene services were notified to attend at Krystal's flat on 20 August 2009, two months after her disappearance. It was put to him that Chantelle Fraser had given evidence that civilians had been allowed into the premises and had washed sheets and clothes before the examination. He said, 'I don't believe it did. I'd be very surprised if it did happen.'

Although a toothbrush, razor and hairbrush were taken from Krystal's flat, Woltsche said no DNA testing had ever been undertaken. He also said that he spoke to Steve Drummond, who led the forensic examination at the flat, who told him there were no signs of forced entry, a struggle, blood, or evidence of a clean up to remove evidence.

* * *

David Toll was subpoenaed and gave evidence at the inquiry. His previous alibi for Peter Jenkinson on the night of Krystal's disappearance was enhanced during his evidence by stating that he recalled that his mate, Jenkinson, had actually stayed later than normal on the night of Krystal's disappearance, his belief then being that Jenkinson had not left his (Toll's) place until midnight.

This testimony was inconsistent with the 11.00 pm time he had told me and the 'before midnight' he had originally disclosed in his statement to homicide investigators in 2009. The implication of a midnight departure unambiguously safeguarded Jenkinson from being in Leitchville at 11.59 pm and making a phone call to Krystal.

Under examination by Fiona Batten, counsel assisting the coroner, his evidence became a little confusing as he then implied that the chess game with Peter Jenkinson he had described may have been on the Friday night (19 June 2009), his belief, at that moment, being that Krystal disappeared in the early hours of the Saturday morning (20 June 2009.)

*   *   *

Counsel representing Peter Jenkinson, Emma Strugnell, applied on his behalf pursuant to section 57 of the Coroners Act — privilege in respect of self-incrimination in other proceedings.

This section applies if a witness objects to giving evidence at an inquest on the grounds that the evidence may tend to prove that the witness has committed an offence. The coroner must have determined there were sufficient grounds for the objection as she approved the application and Jenkinson was excused from giving evidence.

*   *   *

I have paraphrased the coroner's findings at the conclusion of the inquest:
- i) Krystal Lee Fraser, born 18 August 1985 is deceased and she died on or shortly after the early hours of 21 June 2009, near Leitchville.
- ii) Krystal did not die of natural causes.
- iii) She did not die of suicide or misadventure.
- iv) Krystal's death was caused by another person.
- v) There is insufficient evidence to conclude that

Mr Jenkinson was responsible for Krystal's death. However, there is no evidence that excludes Mr Jenkinson as a person who may have been involved in her death.

vi) The caller from the Leitchville phone box was involved in Krystal's disappearance and it follows that Mr Jenkinson, as the caller, was involved in what happened to Krystal after she was taken to the Leitchville area and has been untruthful to police about it.

vii) It is highly probable that the caller was involved in transporting Krystal from her unit in Pyramid Hill to an area near Patho and then to an area near Leitchville. (The coroner also recorded, 'It is notable that the telephone records show that at 12.30 am on 21 June 2009, Mr Jenkinson checked his voice mail messages and his mobile was connected to the network via the Patho tower. These records indicate that Mr Jenkinson was awake and not at home at around the time that Krystal's mobile was on the move from Pyramid Hill to Patho.'

viii) The circumstantial evidence before the court satisfies me to the required civil standard that Mr Jenkinson was involved in her disappearance. There are inconsistencies in Mr Jenkinson's explanations about key matters concerning his relationship with Krystal and her disappearance.

Chapter Twenty-Five   Coronial Inquest

ix) Mr Jenkinson was not able to account for his whereabouts on the evening of 20 June 2009.

x) Mr Jenkinson gave untruthful and inconsistent answers about his sexual relationship with Krystal. He admitted to police to having sex with Krystal a few times three years earlier and denied it when discussing her with former detective Mr Kristic.

xi) Mr Jenkinson admitted to his friend Stephen Jones that he had been having sex with Krystal for the previous two years.

xii) Evidence established that Mr Jenkinson had a sexual relationship with Krystal which was continuing at the time of her conception.

xiii) Significance of the extensive phone calls between Mr Jenkinson and Krystal between 1 January 2008 and 13 May 2009 following which there were no calls between them and the calls to Krystal beginning from the Leitchville public phone was noted. The coroner found this was done to conceal his contact with her before she disappeared after which he immediately ceased calling her from the phone box.

There is an error in the coroner's findings in relation to item vii) above. Tim Miller, the Telstra specialist gave evidence at the inquest in relation to the whereabouts of Peter Jenkinson's mobile at various times. His evidence was that Jenkinson's mobile 'pinged' off the Patho tower at 12.38

am on 20 June 2009 and not on 21 June 2009 as recorded by the coroner.

The coroner raised this as a rather crucial point. The fact that she falsely believed Jenkinson was out and about during the period that Krystal was believed to have been collected from her flat was consequential. I would contend that the coroner's mistake in relation to this issue would not have affected her findings, had she known, as she had sufficient cogent evidence before her to determine Jenkinson's responsibility for Krystal's disappearance.

The coroner made no adverse finding in respect of Victoria Police or Bendigo Health. She did however concede, with the benefit of hindsight, that if Victoria Police had immediately been aware that Krystal had been the victim of foul play, its investigation may have had a different focus from the outset. Instead, local police responded to information reports indicating Krystal was alive and with friends.

The coroner reflected, however, that a differently focused investigation would not have resulted in Krystal being found alive as the evidence strongly indicated that she died soon after she received the midnight call from the Leitchville phone box.

CHAPTER TWENTY-SIX

Conclusion

Krystal Lee Fraser disappeared from her home town of Pyramid Hill shortly after receiving a call originating from the Leitchville phone box at 11.59 pm on Saturday 20 June 2009. The whereabouts of the 23-year-old expectant mother remains unknown. A reasonable inference, regrettably, is that she met with foul play and is dead.

Her disappearance followed her self-discharge from the maternity accommodation wing of the Bendigo Hospital shortly after 6.00 pm that day. Nursing staff were critical of her departure but powerless to prevent it.

Krystal's decision to leave the hospital followed the receipt of a phone call at 5.42 pm from the same Leitchville phone box; Krystal telling staff she had been invited to a party that evening. Enquiries have failed to establish whether there was a party or the caller used the prospect of a party to entice Krystal to return to Pyramid Hill. Whatever the actual reason there was clearly a link between the person calling from the phone box and Krystal's homecoming. It was widely accepted among investigators that verifying the identity of the individual using the phone box would reveal Krystal's killer.

Although fully aware of the imminent birth of Krystal's first child, her mother Karen, who was running the family's confectionary business out of Horsham with her husband Neil, was consumed by Neil's health at the time. He had been hospitalised suffering from pancreatitis. Compounding Karen's concerns was the fact that they had been unable to operate their family business with Neil incapacitated, and this was jeopardising its very existence.

Despite her anxieties, Karen tried to maintain contact with Krystal throughout this critical time. She was relieved when Krystal was admitted to hospital on Tuesday 16 June to have her baby. She was surprised but not alarmed to learn that Krystal had caught the train back to Pyramid Hill on the following Friday, accepting that Krystal was capable of this type of impulsive behaviour. Krystal rang her mum on the Saturday morning telling her that she had been returned to Bendigo Hospital by ambulance late the previous night and this had put her mind at rest.

When Karen rang her again that evening and suspected that Krystal was at the Bendigo railway station and said as much she was alarmed at the level of Krystal's anger over the suggestion, assuming she must have got it wrong.

As a result of Neil Fraser's hospitalisation and the risks facing their business, Karen decided she would undertake the confectionary run with the assistance of her younger daughter,

Chantel, who was living with her parents in Horsham at the time. Karen had not spoken to Krystal since the previous Saturday night but was not concerned as Krystal was, as far as she was concerned, in hospital. When she was unable to contact Krystal on the Sunday or Monday Karen assumed that Krystal must have flattened her phone battery and have left her charger at home, as she had regularly done in the past.

When Karen and Chantel received a call from a Bendigo Hospital midwife looking for Krystal late on the Tuesday morning, they were at a loss, having believed Krystal was an inpatient there. They learned of Krystal's departure from the hospital the preceding Saturday night and her subsequent failure to return. Karen arranged for Neil's mother, Helen Fraser, to visit Krystal's flat to look for her.

Karen and Chantel headed to Pyramid Hill in the confectionary truck and went to Krystal's flat to make their own enquiries. They then attended at the local police station to report Krystal missing after failing to find any trace of her. Pressed for time and conscious of her night blindness, Karen headed to Wedderburn in the truck with Chantel planning to report Krystal as a missing person there as the Pyramid Hill cop had been uncontactable. However, while en route, she decided that making the report at Pyramid Hill where Krystal was well known was a better option. Karen tasked Helen Fraser with this and she made the report to Sen-Constable Jason Brady at the local police station later that day.

Brady, the responsible member, said he took the report

seriously, submitting the missing person's report and notifying his superiors and the criminal investigation unit in Bendigo on the day of the report. He indicated that his initial steps involved attendance at the Bendigo hospital, liaison with hospital management and viewing CCTV footage at both the hospital and the Bendigo railway station. He said he also attended at the block of flats in which Krystal's was located and made enquiries with her neighbours. My enquiries established that he failed to canvass any of the neighbours living directly across the street from Krystal's flat. It seems he wasn't alone in this regard based on my discussions with these residents.

Brady stated that he was fully aware before Krystal's disappearance that the Department of Human Services was involved and that Krystal had been told by the agency that it was going to take her baby. He maintains he had been told this by DHS and that Karen and Krystal both knew it, adding that Krystal had even been telling people around town this. These comments are inconsistent with those of the DHS child protection officer responsible for Krystal's case and were not supported by anyone else I spoke to. The case officer said her department engaged in a monitoring and support role during the later stages of Krystal's pregnancy and there had never been a suggestion the agency would remove the baby. This officer said both Karen and Krystal Fraser were aware of this and of Krystal's requirement to attend a five-day course following the birth, during which she would be taught parenting skills and her progress monitored.

The CPO insists that there was not only no suggestion of the removal of Krystal's baby, but there had also been no in-house discussion about the possibility. The CPO also disclosed that the only conversation she had with police in relation to Krystal was after her disappearance and that during that exchange there had no discussion about the possibility of taking Krystal's baby. The CPO said that she never spoke to a Jason Brady of Pyramid Hill police station.

If Brady knew that Krystal's baby was going to be taken before her disappearance, why didn't he tell Helen Fraser this when she made the initial missing person's report, rather than suggesting that Krystal had simply travelled to Horsham to catch up with her father in hospital? Similarly, why did he never share or discuss this information with Krystal's parents, particularly when Karen Fraser was constantly telling him that Krystal hadn't simply taken off?

It appears that Brady's first entry to Krystal's flat followed prompting from Karen Fraser, an entry effected with the assistance of local CFA member Mark Lacey by the removal of a fly screen. Lacey recalled that Brady locked the premises upon their departure with a key he found within the flat. Brady, however, was vague about this entry, maintaining that whenever he went to Krystal's flat he was in the presence of the police officer from Serpentine and a member of the Fraser family who supplied the key.

The Frasers deny that they had a key, saying that it was Brady who opened the flat when they went there together and that the Serpentine officer, known to the family, was never present. Whatever the circumstances, there is evidence that Krystal's flat was either not secured or not protected from contamination. What is clear is that Krystal's flat, including her clothing and bedding, was cleaned by well-meaning locals before being forensically examined. There was also the geneticist's missing report, which may have provided proof of paternity of Krystal's baby, and the apparent removal of a photograph from Krystal's album.

If Brady had conducted a thorough examination of Krystal's flat from the outset, as his position obliged, and Krystal's wallet was found, his fixation that Krystal was simply in hiding may have shifted dramatically, conceivably resulting in an urgent criminal investigation. Brady said that he did change his attitude about Krystal being in hiding when records of calls to and from her mobile were obtained by detectives later.

Brady claimed that Bendigo CIU detectives were in Pyramid Hill within three days of the report being made. This is not supported by the facts. Detective Mark Crossley, formerly of Bendigo CIU, told the coroner he was first briefed on 21 July 2009 and conducted a search of Krystal's flat the following day.

Despite their involvement, it is difficult to understand why they weren't in contact with the Fraser family, which they weren't. Karen Fraser is adamant that the only contact with this group was when one of its members rang her and apologised for not being aware of the family's existence, telling her that Brady had not informed them. He also alluded to the fact that Brady had encouraged them to accept that Krystal was simply in hiding.

In evidence given at the inquest Crossley confirmed this view, telling the court '...there was a significant emphasis that Krystal had run away.' Despite the involvement of the Bendigo CIU, Brady was still being quoted in media coverage as late as 8 August.

Why was the CIU not being referenced in the media by this stage? Crossley's evidence was that they obtained CCRs on Krystal's phone by the end of the first week of their involvement at the end of July and reverse CCRs in the first week of August 2009.

The earliest public recognition that Krystal may have been murdered coincided with an announcement on 15 October that the homicide squad had taken over Krystal's investigation. Troubling was the comment attributed to the lead investigator that his squad had taken over the investigation despite the fact that no new evidence had been uncovered. Was this an acknowledgement that they should have been involved from the outset?

It seems pretty clear by this stage that investigators had information from Carlo Anfuso, the young tradie who had interacted with Krystal on a chat line, concerning a threat made to Krystal by the father of her baby. The nature of the threat alleged to have been that he would kill Krystal if she gave birth to the baby.

The parallel focus of both the Bendigo CIU and homicide investigators was on identifying the 'mystery' caller understood to have been using the Leitchville phone box to call Krystal. Analysis of Krystal's phone records, and presumably many others identified through this process, along with scrutiny of calls made from the public phone, obviously established a number of potential suspects.

Police enquiries made as a result established that Krystal had been involved with a number of intimate partners before her disappearance. It has been confirmed that at least four men were arrested or interviewed as persons of interests. These were Steve Jones, Craig Newton, Jason McPherson and Peter Jenkinson. Four others were named during the inquest, three of whom gave evidence, the fourth being deceased, but none were ever considered serious suspects.

After the missing persons squad assumed responsibility for Krystal's disappearance, it embarked on a fresh investigation in 2019 targeting Craig 'Twiggy' Newton. The basis for its probe centred on fresh information provided by a former friend of a Cohuna drug supplier, who verified and added to her allegations. As part of their examination, detectives reviewed intelligence provided to Crimestoppers early on in the initial enquiry. This was material apparently ignored or unknown to homicide personnel during their investigation.

This led them to John Crane and the subsequent covert recording of conversations between Newton and Crane. These conversations may have fostered suspicions against Newton but did not provide any direct evidence against him. Newton, it could be said, was dragged through the ringer by the missing persons squad's unproductive scrutiny.

Det-Sgt Wayne Woltsche, who led the homicide squad investigation, had resolved that Peter Jenkinson was the person responsible for Krystal's disappearance and he informed the Fraser family of this.

The suspicion levelled against Jenkinson was based on several factors. Jenkinson and Krystal had been in regular phone contact for a lengthy period of time, communication via their mobiles and Jenkinson's landline that appeared to have ended on 13 May 2009, thirty-seven days before Krystal's disappearance. Immediately following the termination of these verified calls between the pair, calls to Krystal started from the Leitchville phone box on 14 May 2009. Telstra records confirmed that Krystal had never received calls from this phone previously.

Krystal's family was also aware that Krystal was meeting a man she referred to as PJ for sex at the base of the hill in Pyramid Hill. Krystal told her sister, Chantel, that PJ had a wife and kids in Gunbower and that was why they had to meet in secret. The fact that Jenkinson had to pay out a former partner to the tune of about $100,000 and was also paying maintenance to a son born to another woman were considered motives for killing Krystal and her baby.

Based on information provided by the Fraser family that Krystal was going to name the baby's father as part of an application for the Baby Bonus and have a DNA test in an attempt to prove paternity, it is highly likely that Jenkinson was aware that Krystal was about to expose their relationship. Contributing to this, no doubt, was Krystal's attempt to get someone to take paternal responsibility for the baby shortly before her disappearance, as revealed by Kerryn Watson.

The revelation of his intimate relationship with a woman with an intellectual disability were likely confronting given that he had gone to lengths to prevent its discovery over a prolonged period of time. The evidence of Alex Kristic concerning the comments alleged to have been made to him by Jenkinson after Krystal's disappearance provide clarity as to Jenkinson's opinion of Krystal, referring to her as '... a bloody drug fucked nuffy.'

Kristic also provides a connection between Jenkinson and Krystal's pregnancy with the alleged comments he attributed to Steve Jones, 'She'd been telling everyone that she was pregnant to Peter and that she was carrying his kid.'

The nature and timing of the final contact between Krystal and Carlo Anfuso should not be viewed in isolation. An alleged threat to kill Krystal by the father of her baby made in the week of her disappearance is extremely relevant. And who of Krystal's numerous intimate partners was she communicating with during this same week? There may have been others, but we know for certain that Peter Jenkinson did by his own admission, with his acknowledgement of a call to Krystal while she was in the Bendigo Hospital, telling homicide investigators he made a call from his mobile.

Homicide investigators established, through Telstra, that there were no calls to Krystal from Jenkinson's mobile or landline at that time. However, there was a call to Krystal from the Leitchville phone box within the period Jenkinson told police he'd rung her from his mobile phone.

Proof of Jenkinson's connection with Krystal during her last week can also be found in Krystal's diary entry of Tuesday 16 June 2009, where she recorded details of a telephone conversation she had just had with him and her expectation of catching up with him on the weekend. Telco records confirm a call to Krystal's mobile at 7.45 pm that day, which was made from the Leitchville phone box and not from Jenkinson's phones. There is a clear inference that this call, albeit an innocuous one, was made by Jenkinson from the Leitchville phone box. Jenkinson admitted to having used the phone box occasionally but never for the purpose of ringing Krystal. Detectives believed this was to cover his tracks in case a forensic examination or witnesses, confirmed his use.

Further corroboration of Jenkinson's use of the Leitchville phone box to contact Krystal is based on the disclosures he is alleged to have made to Sen-Constable Chris Goyne, the former officer in charge of Gunbower police station. Goyne made notes of a brief exchange he had with Jenkinson nine days after Krystal's disappearance in which Jenkinson acknowledged the Tuesday (16 June 2009) night call to Krystal and told him that he had also rung Krystal at the Bendigo hospital on the Thursday or Friday (18 or 19 June 2009) from his mobile.

Again, records show that there were no calls made from his mobile to Krystal on these days but there were two calls from the Leitchville phone box on Friday 19 June 2009, the day before Krystal's disappearance.

Who knew Krystal would be returning to Pyramid Hill on the weekend of her disappearance? There were five calls made from the phone box at Leitchville to Krystal following her admission to hospital on 16 June. The one at 7.45 pm, the two on Friday 19 June, one while Krystal was at the hospital and the other after her return to Pyramid Hill that night. The final two calls were made on the day of her disappearance, the first being the origin of the claimed invitation to a party late on the Saturday afternoon and the definitive one just before midnight. A total of five calls made to Krystal from this phone over a period of five days.

Assuming that there was only one person using this service to contact Krystal, this caller had knowledge of Krystal's return. On the basis of Krystal's diary notation about having just spoken to her good mate PJ and hoping to catch up with him on the weekend, Jenkinson's acknowledgment of calls to her and the evidence provided by telco records, there is a strong presumption that Peter Jenkinson was the person using the phone box on both 16 and 19 June and was aware of her imminent return to Pyramid Hill.

Within this context is it also reasonable to suspect that Peter Jenkinson was responsible for all these calls?

It should be pointed out that investigators have confirmed that telco records established that Peter Jenkinson never again rang Krystal's mobile following her disappearance. Similarly, the phone box at Leitchville was never used again after the 11.59 pm call on Saturday 20 June 2009 to ring Krystal's mobile. It follows that the person who had been using the phone box to communicate with Krystal was fully aware that she could not receive any further calls.

Also incriminating, if allowed in evidence, is Peter Jenkinson's alleged statement made after his release and picked up on the illegal bug planted in his vehicle of, 'Fuck, they got me. Nah, fuck it, they won't get me.'

Then there is the evidence of Steve Jones' daughter, Shannon, who said she overheard Peter Jenkinson telling her father that he would have to kill Krystal, essentially because he wanted her to get rid of her baby, which he believed was his, and she had refused; and her father trying to talk him out of it. Shannon's testimony also provides further corroboration of Jenkinson's feelings for Krystal when he is overheard using the identical terminology to describe her as used when discussing her with Alex Kristic, referring to her as a 'nuffy'. Shannon also said that she overheard Jenkinson telling her father that Krystal had rung him and, '...wanted him at the hospital, but he'd said no.' This is critical evidence that Shannon claimed detectives refused to receive in 2009 until missing persons squad officers were encouraged to revisit her in 2022 following their visit to my house.

Do the actions of Steve Jones in having an intense argument with Peter Jenkinson in the main street of Gunbower following the news of Krystal's disappearance and searching for Krystal and evidence against the person responsible, support Shannon's observations? It lends credibility to her statement.

There is evidence that the two men were very close ahead of Krystal's disappearance. David Toll, the former lawyer who provided the alibi for Jenkinson, also confirmed a close relationship between Jenkinson and Jones that deteriorated to a point where, he said, Jones pulled a gun on Jenkinson. This assertion was also made by Steve Jones' former wife Denise. What brought about the massive change in their relationship?

The original alibi offered to investigators for Jenkinson by Toll was that Jenkinson left his place before midnight on the night of Krystal's disappearance. This became 11.00 pm when I spoke to him and 10.00 pm when later spoken to by missing persons squad detectives.

While Toll reverted to the original time of midnight during his evidence at the inquest, his testimony was such that it does not adequately safeguard Jenkinson as an alibi is designed to. Given the weakness in his alibi, Jenkinson is not shielded from having made the final phone call to Krystal from the Leitchville phone box at 11.59 pm.

Another disconcerting aspect of the alibi is that Toll had said his wife was in hospital having tests on this night and that Jenkinson and he were the only ones at his home that night. Toll's wife challenged this, having responded that she was home. Another troubling feature of the alibi is that Toll's wife did not know her husband had provided one. It should also be noted that Peter Jenkinson has been unable to provide proof of his whereabouts between midnight on 20 June and 2.49 am on 21 June 2009.

The killer planned to get rid of Krystal and her baby before the baby's birth, either believing the baby was his or that he would be saddled with accountability for it. It is possible Krystal contributed to this belief in her efforts to find a father for her baby. Again, the evidence of Carlo Anfuso, Shannon Jones and Kerryn Watson reinforce this theory.

How can Peter Jenkinson be considered the killer of Krystal and her unborn baby when Krystal was referring to him in her diary entry of 16 June 2009, a few days before her disappearance, as her 'good mate?' This is a man, overheard by Chantel Fraser, crudely hounding Krystal for money the month before, prompting Krystal's exodus from Pyramid Hill to avoid him shortly after her family had returned from Horsham for the weekend.

What brought about his changed attitude towards Krystal, or at least Krystal's perception of their relationship? Had he given Krystal assurances that he would take responsibility for her baby in response to her requests? But how does that meld with their decision to stop ringing one another from their personal phones about five weeks before her disappearance? How was he able to convince Krystal to stop ringing him? Why was she so firm in this resolve? What inspired this great self-control in a seemingly impulsive young woman? What was in it for Krystal? It can be argued that she believed there was something she dearly craved — a father for her baby.

Finally, there is the violence Jenkinson is alleged to have later committed against his former partner, particularly that following the *Herald Sun*'s front page coverage of Krystal's disappearance and the offer of a million-dollar reward on 17 July 2019. It is plausible that pressure was building on Jenkinson around this time with police divers and drone activity on the boundary of his property and the thrust of the article being about 'new information' being received about a person previously spoken to in the investigation.

It is recognised that Krystal's intellectual disability, resulting from hydrocephalus, made decision making difficult. These cognitive difficulties were dealt with by a loving family and supportive teachers until she completed high school. Krystal didn't want to be restricted by rules imposed by others by this time and began to rebel.

After moving into her own flat at age nineteen, Krystal began a series of intimate relationships with men described by her mother as 'lowlifes.' Karen Fraser said she was critical of Krystal's choices in men and would often tell her daughter this. Krystal began to tell her family less about these men, Karen suspects through fear of further reproach. Some of the men Krystal was associating with by this time were involved in drug dealing. By her own admissions, she was couriering drugs on the train for them, telling both her mother and grandmother that the dealers had told her that she wouldn't get into trouble if she got caught because she was a 'nuffer.'

The men she associated with were clearly ruthless types. Krystal named PJ as one of these dealers. It should be noted that there is no evidence to support these allegations other than through reports of Krystal's unproven disclosures.

Criticism by her family of Krystal's relationships may be interpreted as the reason she failed to tell her mother that she was returning to Pyramid Hill on the night of her disappearance, knowledge that may have enabled Karen to save Krystal's life. This exaggerates her family's influence as Krystal had been living fully independently for some time by this stage, with her parents residing in Horsham.

This supposition about Krystal's reason for keeping her final return to Pyramid Hill secret also underestimates the level of control that Peter Jenkinson exercised over her. There was clearly a power imbalance in their relationship, with Krystal responding to phone calls and having to walk to a given location to be picked up and taken to the picnic area at 'the hill' for sex. She was not to talk about the relationship as he spuriously, 'had a wife and kids in Gunbower and couldn't be seen picking her up from her flat.' And there is the unsubstantiated allegation that he had her running drugs for him.

Calls to Krystal at the hospital, made from the Leitchville phone box, were to ensure her return to Pyramid Hill before the baby was born so that the killer could achieve his purpose. It is credible that his plans were disrupted following Krystal's return to town on the Friday when she visited her grandmother and also spent hours at the local pub. Too many people being aware that she was home increased the killer's risk of exposure.

Remember the evidence of Melodee Hose who was at the Pyramid Hill pub on the night of 19 June 2009 when Krystal told her, "I'm waiting for my mate to call" and said that Krystal leaned into her as she said it, '… like it was a bit of a secret.' Interesting perhaps that Krystal was waiting for '… my mate,' the same portrayal she recorded in her diary three days earlier to describe Peter Jenkinson.

To ensure his plans could be achieved the killer made sure that Krystal returned to town late on the Saturday, likely instructing her not to tell anyone about their scheduled meeting. Hence the intensity of Krystal's lie to Karen about not being at the Bendigo railway station awaiting the train. This was not a case of Krystal avoiding her mother's criticism but one of keeping a secret as directed to by her killer.

The story the killer dished up to Krystal about a local party was cunning for if her disappearance was established quickly enquiries would have initially been undertaken to identify the location of the party. It would have bought him time. This became unnecessary, however, as the murderer's cause was aided by the actions of Sen-Constable Jason Brady and his erroneous insistence that Krystal was simply in hiding. In his defence, however, the nature and circumstances surrounding Krystal's disappearance should have rung alarm bells throughout Victoria Police from the outset.

Even if Brady's superiors failed to acknowledge the gravity of Krystal's disappearance, regional detectives should have enquired into the matter. The absurd thirty-day rule that Mark Crossley of Bendigo CIU spoke of, which compelled his office to make enquiries after Krystal had been missing for that length of time, while eventually compelling action, it effectively impeded an appropriate and timely response.

The coroner, while acknowledging Peter Jenkinson's denials and the absence of any physical evidence of what happened to Krystal, determined that the circumstantial evidence satisfied her 'to the required civil standard' that Jenkinson was involved in Krystal's disappearance. She has forwarded a report to the Office of Public Prosecutions (OPP) specifying that she believes Peter Jenkinson is responsible for an indictable (serious) offence in relation to the death of Krystal Fraser. The missing persons squad has also delivered a brief of evidence to the OPP for consideration of a charge of murder against Jenkinson.

The delay in resolving the circumstances of Krystal's

disappearance and the lack of publicity afforded the case compared to many others, raises an important question: did the stigma attached to Krystal because of her disability, the issue that marginalised her through life, also impact on the quality of the investigation into her death?

BIBLIOGRAPHY

1. Victoria Police Manual, *Reporting missing persons and managing missing persons investigations,* 22/02/2010
2. Online Continuing Education for the Professional Investigator, *Locating Mobile Phones Through Pinging and Triangulation* 1 July 2008
3. National Institute of Neurological Disorders and Stroke, National Institute of Health, *"Hydrocephalus Fact Sheet",* Bethesda, 31/05/2020
4. Family Planning NSW Factsheet *Contraceptive implants* June 2018
5. Canberra Institute of Criminology, *Domestic/family homicide in Australia,* Canberra 2015
6. National Disability Authority – Centre for Excellence in Universal Design, *"Disability Overview",* 2014, Dublin
7. New York Times, *US Domestic Violence,* 2019/04/12
8. Research article BMC Psychiatry 16 Australia, *"A case study into crime and victimisation in people with intellectual disability,* 2016, Fogden, BC, Thomas, SDM, Daffern, M & Ogloff, JRP
9. Crime Statistics Agency *Recorded criminal incidents year ending 2019.*

10. Disability Studies: Quarterly, *Relationship Depth and Associative Stigma of Disability,* Vol 37, No.3, Nieweglowski, K, & Sheehan L, Chicago 2017.
11. Sydney Morning Herald 19/01/2009
12. Ugur Nedim, Principal of Sydney Criminal Lawyers, website 2020.
13. *Egyptian Journal of Forensic Sciences* Vol 3–4, Sep-Dec 2011, pages 140–143, Madani, O, Kjoroshah, Youseff, M, Moulana, A.
14. *American journal of forensic medicine and pathology*, Official publication of the National Association of Medical Examiners, 28(4), pages 288–291, Blumenthal, R.
15. Healthy Debates, *The suicide gap: why men are more likely to die from suicide than women*, 10/08/2017, Milne, J, Tepper, J, Pelch, J.
16. Victoria University Melbourne, Evidence LLW4007 – *Evidence improperly or illegally obtained* 2020
17. *Geographic profiling*, CRC Press, 1999 Washington DC
18. www.mobiletowerguide.com.au
    Powertec Telecommunications Pty Ltd, Southport, Qld 2015
19. NRI.TAMU, Education Blog, *Wild pig and human interaction,* 3/1/2019
20. www.sciencealert.com. 31/3/2016

www.ingramcontent.com/pod-product-compliance
Lightning Source LLC
Chambersburg PA
CBHW041135110526
44590CB00027B/4028